MATERIALIZED APPARITIONS • BRACKETT, EDWARD AUGUSTUS

Introduction, Page 9 2

Part I.
MATERIALIZATION AND DEMATERIALIZATION
OF FORMS AND OBJECTS.
CHAPTER. PAGE.
I. My First Séance, and What Came of It 17 2

II. Personification by the Medium, or Materialized Forms? 30 4

III. Materialization and Dematerialization of Objects 36 5

IV. Materialization and Dematerialization under Test Conditions 51 7

V. An Unexpected Séance 60 8

VI. Séance with Mrs. Carrie M. Sawyer 68 9

VII. Séances with Mrs. Fairchild 79 . 11

VIII. Séance with Miss Helen Berry at Onset 88 12

IX. Séance at the Berry Sisters' in Boston 99 13

X. Materialized Forms—How shall We Meet Them? 109 15

Part II.
OPINIONS AND THEORIES.
I. A Glance Behind the Curtain 123 .. 16

II. Exposures of Mediums 131 17

III. Public Séances 140 18

IV. The Attitude of Scientists 146 19

V. Public Opinion 153 20

VI. Conclusion 164 21

ILLUSTRATIONS.
Diagram of Mrs. Fay's Séance-Room 29 4

Diagram of the Misses Berry's Séance-Room 100 14

Publisher's Note
Purchase of this book entitles you to a free trial membership in the publisher's book club at www.rarebooksclub.com. (Time limited offer.) Simply enter the barcode number from the back cover onto the membership form on our home page. The book club entitles you to select from millions of books at no additional charge. You can also download a digital copy of this and related books to read on the go. Simply enter the title or subject onto the search form to find them.

Note: This is an historic book. Pages numbers, where present in the text, refer to the first edition of the book and may also be in indexes.

If you have any questions, could you please be so kind as to consult our Frequently Asked Questions page at www.rarebooksclub.com/faqs.cfm? You are also welcome to contact us there.
Publisher: General Books LLC™, Memphis, TN, USA, 2012. ISBN: 9781151356925.
Proofreading: pgdp.net

Materialized Apparitions
Materialized Apparitions
If Not Beings from Another Life What Are They
BY
EDWARD A. BRACKETT
Author of "The World We Live In", "My House," Etc.
BOSTON
RICHARD G. BADGER
The Gorham Press
1908

Copyright 1885, by E. A. Brackett
All Rights Reserved
The Gorham Press, Boston, U. S. A.
To abandon these spiritual phenomena to credulity, is to commit a treason against human reason. Nevertheless, we see them always rejected and always reappearing. They date not their advent from yesterday.
Victor Hugo.

PREFACE.
Written at intervals from the pressure of business, and at times that should have been devoted to recreation, these pages make no claim to artistic arrangement

or literary merit. If they enable any one to arrive at a clearer and better appreciation of the wonderful phenomena of which they treat, they will have accomplished all that was intended.

Winchester, Mass.

[9] INTRODUCTION.

In 1840 I became acquainted with Dr. Colyer, then lecturing on Mesmerism, at Peel's Museum, New York, and fully believed, at that time, that he was a humbug, and Mesmerism a fraud. Soon after this, while visiting some friends, with Mr. Pendleton, formerly from Boston, this subject was pretty thoroughly discussed,—Mr. Pendleton insisting that there was truth in it, and that I was not treating it fairly; and he proposed, as a matter of amusement, that I should try the experiment on some one of the party present. Willing to turn the discussion into a less serious form, I consented to take the part assigned me; and soon found, to my astonishment, that I had before me a most excellent clairvoyant subject. What had been started as amusement became a very interesting entertainment, resulting in the [10] meeting of the parties once a week for the purpose of studying Mesmerism.

In the following spring I removed to Boston, where in my leisure hours I continued my investigations, part of the time with Dr. William F. Channing, the inventor of the Fire Alarm, and at the time a student with Dr. Jackson. I was indebted to him for many interesting suggestions, and especially for the use of a very delicate galvanometer, for the purpose of detecting, if possible, any magnetic or electric currents passing between the magnetizer and his subject. No such currents were discovered, and when we found that our subject could be controlled and thrown into a trance when more than a mile away, by the action of the will alone, the idea of testing currents was abandoned. All that has since been made public under the names of Mind-Reading and Telepathy, and much more, was familiar to us.

When trance-mediumship became known, believing that it was only a form of Mesmerism, I gave considerable attention to it. There were few mediums of note that I did not have more or less sittings with, but the most satisfactory [11] communications I received came through a member of my own family. While the evidence was such as would have convinced most persons that these messages came from the other side of life, I was by no means sure of it.

In this state of mind, in consequence of some statements made to me by Mr. Thomas Appleton, of what he had seen in Europe, I decided to investigate what is known as "Materialization," that is, the alleged production of visible and tangible apparitions out of seeming nothingness. I felt, whether right or wrong, that my experience in Mesmerism, and the long training of my perceptive faculties as a sculptor, which enabled me to detect the slightest differences between objects, was as good a preparation as one could have for studying this class of phenomena. I had no sectarian prejudices to overcome, and no lack of courage in stating my convictions, no matter which way the evidence might lead. That I prejudged the case in the beginning, I freely admit, and, like thousands of others, formed an opinion without giving to it that attention which is necessary in dealing fairly with any subject.

[12] I have a thorough abhorrence of fraud, whether in the séance-room or in the pulpit, regarding any one who would trifle with the most sacred feelings of our nature as deserving the severest punishment.

In briefly detailing some of the facts that have come under my own observation, it is a matter of no consequence to me what may be said about them, since it is impossible for any one to give the subject the same careful study without arriving at similar results.

[13] Part I.
MATERIALIZATION AND DEMATERIALIZATION OF FORMS AND OBJECTS.
[14]

[15] Man is what he feels. He may dazzle the world for a while with the splendor of his acquirements, but, like an iceberg that glistens in the frosty air and disappears in a more genial clime, the pride of his intellect is lost in the warmth of his affections.

What Swedenborg aptly terms his "loves," alone indicate man's true character. They determine his relation to superior as well as to inferior beings. There is no other way through which he can advance to a higher life, or commune with those exalted spirits who are ever ready to welcome him, than by the elevation of his affections. Through every phase of his spiritual progress, whether in this or the other life, forever arches over him in letters of gold the divine commandment, "That ye love one another." [16]

[17] MATERIALIZED APPARITIONS.

CHAPTER I.
MY FIRST SÉANCE, AND WHAT CAME OF IT.

Not being acquainted with any "materializing medium," so termed, I obtained from Mr. Luther Colby, of Boston, a letter of introduction to Mrs. H. B. Fay, of that city, stating that I was desirous of visiting her séances. I called upon the lady and presented the letter, but found that she was out of health, and, for the present, had discontinued her sittings. I, however, left my address, with the request that she would inform me when she resumed her séances.

[18] More than a year passed without hearing from her, and, finding that she was giving sittings, I made free to call at the house and ask admittance, which was granted. As she did not recognize me, I felt confident that she had forgotten the circumstance of the letter, and, as I preferred to remain as far as possible *incog.*, I made no allusion to it.

Curiosity led me to scan the audience. There were about thirty persons present, and, as far as I could judge, they were of more than ordinary intelligence. At the beginning of the séance, the light was lowered, but not so low that we could not discern clearly the features of those around us.

I do not propose now to deal with the experience of others, although I have from the beginning made that a part of my study, but shall confine myself to what came to me.

[19] Near the close of the séance, the lady who sat next the cabinet said there was a form present who gave the name of "Maggie Brackett." She would not be certain about the first name, as the form was very weak and spoke in a whisper. Here was a chance to come in contact with one of these beings, supposed to belong to another life. Although I knew of no one, in or out of my family, by that name, I assumed that it was for me, and stepped up to the cabinet. As I did so, the curtain parted, and a very beautiful female, apparently about sixteen years old, stood before me. I looked at her very closely, but could trace no resemblance to the medium, nor to any one I had known. I said, "I do not remember you; did I ever see you before?" She shook her head, and tried to speak, but I could not make out what she intended to say.

Finding that I did not understand, she [20] held out her hand, about three feet from the floor; but I did not know what that meant, and, seeing that she was greatly disappointed, shook hands with her, saying, "Never mind; we will find out about this some other time;" then bade her Good-bye, and she stepped behind the curtain.

As I turned to my seat, a hoarse voice inside the cabinet somewhat startled me by saying, "Your wife is here!" I answered, "Very well, I shall be glad to see her."

If I was disappointed in the first form, I was doubly so in this. It was a much smaller person than my deceased wife, and had a tired, careworn expression, while the features strongly resembled the medium. She greeted me warmly. Holding her at arms' length, in order to better study her form, I said, "You are not tall or stout enough for my wife. " "Wait," [21] she said; and, stepping behind the curtain, returned in a few moments, fuller, and near a head taller. The height and general build of the form were now very good, but the face was a medley. I saw, or fancied, some resemblance to my wife, but still more to the medium.

She appeared overjoyed at meeting me; so much so that I felt it would be heartless on my part to repel it. Laying her head upon my shoulder, she talked freely with me, saying things that it seemed impossible that any one but my wife could know. I knew what Mesmerism and clairvoyance meant. Was this another phase of them? Was it mind-reading? If so, it was a very clever performance. I could not realize that I had my wife before me, and yet here was a being who had penetrated the inmost secrets of my domestic life; had dragged from the past the well-worn pages of memory and read them anew.

[22] She remained out much longer than most of the forms had done, when I noticed that she appeared to be growing weaker, and, in spite of her efforts to sustain herself, was sinking downward. Bidding her Good-night, I let go her hand. As I did so, she went down directly in front of me, within a foot of where I stood, her head and shoulders being the last part visible. On the carpet, where she disappeared, there was a glow of phosphorescent light, which gradually faded away.

For the first and only time during my investigations, I was unduly excited. It came so suddenly and unexpectedly upon me that I was confused. I brushed my hand across my forehead and eyes to make sure of my bearings, and slowly returned to my seat, fully conscious of the importance of what had passed before me. If real,—if the form had thus dematerialized,—then [23] the reality of materialization followed as a matter of course.

While turning these thoughts over in my mind, the séance closed; and as I stepped out into the full light of the autumnal moon, everything seemed changed. The sound of feet on the brick pavement grated harshly on my ears; before me rose the tall spire of the stone church, throwing its ghostly shadow across the way; behind me was the séance-room, and a dreamy consciousness of the strange phenomena I had witnessed surged through my brain. Was it possible that I had stood face to face and been in communication with one from another life?

As I pondered over this, a reaction came, and before I reached my home the probability, or the possibility even, that I had been deceived, vexed and annoyed me, and aroused a determination to know whether or not there was truth in materialization. [24] I was not overpleased with what I had seen, and, but for this last incident, my investigations might have ended here. Materialization was either a great truth or a stupendous humbug. Thousands of intelligent persons believed in it, on what appeared to me uncertain evidence. Was it not a disgrace to science that this had been allowed to go on so long without any honest attempt to investigate it? If I could only get the inside track, how easy it would be to expose it! The whole thing lay in a nutshell: either the forms appearing were confederates, or personations by the medium; perhaps both. I would if possible adopt a system of investigation so thorough that nothing should escape me.

To go to séances as an ordinary visitor was, to me, to throw time away. If the manifestations were genuine, and my personal relations with the medium not objectionable, [25] I saw no reason why I should not obtain privileges without which, to my skeptical mind, it would be useless to pursue the subject.

I therefore continued my visits, having this object constantly in view. Otherwise I remained perfectly passive, neither demanding nor asking anything.

Several times I was surprised by finding thoughts to which I had given no outward expression anticipated by what claimed to be "the control," that is, the spirit alleged to hold possession of the entranced medium. I had not asked, although greatly desirous, to be taken into the cabinet during the séance. While thinking this, "Auntie," Mrs. Fay's "control," said, "You shall come in."

The forms were coming quite freely to me, and one said, "You may go in with me." As I entered, the control greeted me in a friendly way, saying that she [26] liked me; that I was a skeptic, but an honest one.

While talking with her, I had my left arm around the waist of the form that took me into the cabinet. With my right hand I reached out and satisfied myself that the medium was sitting in her chair, entranced. There could be no mistake; there were four of us in the cabinet,—the two forms that appeared to be materialized, the medium, and myself!

I know how two got in, but where did the other two come from?

Taking advantage of the expressions of kindness on the part of the control, I sought an early opportunity to express to the medium what I desired. To my surprise, she made no objections, saying that she was entranced, and did not know what the forms were, nor was she conscious of taking any part in what came before the audience; that she was simply the instrument, [27] not the operator. I thanked her, saying I trusted that I should do nothing which would be distasteful to her or the control; that the first step would be a thorough investigation of the cabinet.

On my first visit to Mrs. Fay's, the cabinet consisted simply of a curtain drawn across the corner of the room. It was soon after changed to a light, portable structure, which could be easily moved to any part of the room.

I had this cabinet moved out, the floor, wall, and everything connected with it thoroughly examined. There was no chance for confederates to be used here. I have since assisted in moving it out for the satisfaction of others, and have seen it placed in the opposite corner of the room, where it remained for weeks without in the least affecting the manifestations. Whatever may be the cause of [28] these phenomena, they are certainly not due to confederates.

I herewith submit a carefully drawn plan of the cabinet and its surroundings, made by a competent architect, who has never seen any of the manifestations, and consequently is not a believer in them.

There could be no doubt; it was impossible for any one to enter the cabinet except through the door of the séance-room, in the presence of the whole audience. To be perfectly sure on this point, I sought and obtained permission to sit next the cabinet, which place I occupied for more than forty sittings. I know that it is impossible to use a confederate in this cabinet without its being instantly detected.

Having settled this so thoroughly that it could not come up as an element of doubt in any future investigations I might make, the next step seemed to be a plain one.
[29]

Diagram of Mrs. Fay's Séance-Room.

[30] CHAPTER II. PERSONIFICATION BY THE MEDIUM, OR MATERIALIZED FORMS?

The forms that came from the cabinet were either personations by the medium, or they were what they purported to be—materializations.

I had, during this time, allowed nothing to pass unnoticed. From forty to sixty forms would often manifest at a séance, apparently of both sexes, and of all ages and sizes, from a little child to extreme old age, each form individualized and complete in itself.

What claimed to be my wife came to me quite often, and so many times disappeared in the way heretofore described, [31] that I was no longer startled by the occurrence, for I had become so familiar with it that I had come to regard it as a natural consequence of her appearance. She not only grew stronger, but the likeness was much improved, and the resemblance to the medium, at times, entirely disappeared.

In my first visits to these séances, I was led, like many others, to attach great importance to the resemblance which these forms might bear to what they claimed to have been when in earth-life. I was constantly looking for it, and have seen many instances where the likeness was so marked that it would have been impossible to mistake it; yet I have learned not to regard it as positive evidence of identity. Whatever they may be, whether from this or the other side of life, there can be no question that they possess the wonderful power of changing their forms at [32] pleasure, as any one at all familiar with them can testify.

I have seen a tall young man, wearing a full beard, claiming to be a brother of the lady with me, while standing before her, one hand on her waist, the other in mine—upon her saying, "I have not seen you since you were a lad; how do you suppose I should know you now?"—stoop, kiss her on the cheek, and raise his roguish face without the beard; at the same time diminishing in size until he was more nearly like the boy she knew.

I have witnessed similar changes outside of the cabinet, in the presence of the audience, quite often.

The mental and moral tone of the audience has more to do with the character of the séance than the medium has. I have, several times, by the action of a strong will, caused the forms to recede from the position which they at first assumed.

[33] Persons, without being fully aware of it, find themselves more or less reflected in these séances. They reap what they sow. Their condition of mind prevents the forms from approaching them.

I have known persons to visit séances many times without receiving any attention; and, on the other hand, I have seen entire strangers, coming from distant parts of the country, who had never before been in a séance-room, receive the most tender demonstrations of affection and recognition.

Sometimes these forms have treated

me to little jokes, that illustrated better than words the information I was seeking; enjoying heartily anything that for a moment seemed to disconcert me.

What claimed to be my niece came to me in a very beautiful illuminated dress. I asked her to appear to me at the next séance dressed in the same way. I took [34] a friend with me to that séance, expecting to astonish him with the wonderful illumination. But, instead of keeping her promise, she came out in a dark dress, such as I had never seen her wear. As my friend had gone up to the cabinet with me, I was greatly disappointed in the way she came, and said, "Bertha, why do you come in this dress?" Placing her right elbow in the palm of her left hand and her index finger on her lip, in a bashful, coquettish way, she said, "I'm in mourning." I said, "For what?" She replied, "I expect I have lost my friend." I said to my companion, "This is something new; I don't understand it." While we were both looking at her, instantly the dark dress disappeared, and she stood before us radiant in her beautiful garments. With a girlish laugh she threw her arms around my neck, kissed me and said, "It is all right now, uncle." The disappearance [35] of the dark dress was quite as marvellous to my friend as the illumination.

I have never been able to detect any fraud, or any indication of it, on the part of Mrs. Fay at these séances; and in the absence of any information which would lead to any other conclusion, I shall hereafter call these forms spirits. That they are not beings belonging to this side of life, I feel certain. What they are, each one must determine for himself.

[36] **CHAPTER III.**
MATERIALIZATION AND DEMATERIALIZATION OF OBJECTS.

The severest tests which I could apply to these manifestations convinced me that not only the forms which surrounded these spirits, but the garments which they wore were "materialized" (that is, made visible and tangible out of previously invisible substances) inside of the cabinet. How this is done we may not comprehend. Emerson says, "The whole world is the flux of matter over the wires of thought to the points or poles where it would build." We only know that here, as in Nature, there must be a germ or starting-point around which the particles [37] aggregate. This is seen in the materialization of objects, which is important as being the only materializations outside the cabinet, and the only ones that we can study.

I have spoken of a beautiful spirit claiming to be my niece, Bertha, that came to me at Mrs. Fay's. In all my attendance there she has never failed to meet me. This did not arise from any understanding or agreement, but seemed to grow up as a natural consequence of the magnetic relations between us. Simple and childlike in her bearing, I have found her remarkably conscientious, intelligent, and affectionate. She comes freely, and in all my intercourse with her I have never found her judgment at fault.

I do not care to discuss the question as to who or what Bertha is; I know she is not the medium, nor a confederate, and that her materialization of objects is genuine. [38] In my long and delightful association with her, extending over more than two years, I have never been able to detect the slightest thing that would lead me to doubt that she is what she claims to be.

No parent ever watched the unfolding of a young life with more interest than I have studied the apparent growth or development of this delightful spirit. It may be that what I have considered her progress arises from the increasing strength gained through her long association with me, enabling her to more freely express herself; for during my acquaintance with her she has seemingly passed from a commonplace person into a remarkable embodiment of intelligence and affection. If I have refrained from expressing the many inspired thoughts and feelings which in her exalted moments she has freely given forth, it is because [39] they are sacred to my own domestic circle. They belong to that centralization of the affections without which life loses its force, and all investigations or attempts to reach these beings are only time thrown away.

As I never saw her before she passed to the other life, I have no means of proving her identity except by what she has told me. Owing to the fact that her family live many hundred miles away, and that I am very forgetful of names, I did not recall, until reminded by others, the existence of any one of that name. She came, at first, very weak, not being able to come out from the cabinet, and spoke in a whisper. She either gave a wrong name, or, what is quite as likely from the difficulty she then had in expressing herself, was misunderstood. This, with my limited experience, led me to regard her appearance, so far as it [40] related to me, a mistake, and I am quite conscious that I treated her coldly. That she felt this indifference on my part was evinced more than once by the expression of her face.

She, however, continued to come whenever I was present, growing stronger each time, apparently demanding recognition, and showing plainly that she did not mean to be put aside for any one. At length I said, "Will you tell me who you are?" She replied, "I am Bertha; you are my uncle; I am your niece;" at the same time holding out her hand about three feet from the floor. As I did not understand this, she subsequently explained it by coming out as a child about four years old, that being the age, as I afterward learned, when she passed to the other life. As I was a stranger to the medium and all present (except one, and that one knew nothing of my relatives), [41] it does not seem probable that the medium could have known anything about her.

The individuality of Bertha is very striking, bearing little or no resemblance to any other materialized form which I have seen. She never comes shrouded in a profusion of drapery; on the contrary, she appears scantily but richly dressed, wearing a short skirt and close-fitting waist, with short sleeves, leaving her finely-rounded arms bare. She never wears a head-dress; her long silken hair floats freely round her shoulders. In form and feature she is the embodiment of girlhood, with a playful disposition which leads her to make amusing remarks, at times, about those who come within her mental atmosphere.

Her figure is compactly built, and well proportioned, with a remarkably fine face, the expression of which, at times, surpasses [42] anything I have ever seen. She is much shorter than the medium, as the following measurements will show:—

Mrs. H. B. Fay, medium, height,	5 ft. 4 in.
Bertha, materialized form, height,	4 ft. 9-1/4 in.
Male form (to Mr. Tallman), height,	5 ft. 9-1/4 in.
Difference between Mrs. Fay and Bertha,	6-3/4 in.
Difference between Mrs. Fay and male form,	5-1/4 in.
Difference between Bertha and male form,	12 in.

These measurements were taken by means of an upright staff with a cross piece at right angles, and I was assisted by a gentleman who is a thorough skeptic. Care was taken to have the forms stand perfectly upright, so that there could be no mistake as to accuracy.

I have given this brief sketch of Bertha as I shall have occasion to allude to her hereafter, for I am greatly indebted to her for much that I have learned about materialization. She has taught me that the ability to communicate intelligently [43] depends upon the use these beings can make of our aromal emanations, or magnetism; that frequent association with us is necessary to enable them to gain control of material elements, and that where the relations are harmonious they gather strength every time they come in contact with us.

From a feeble and almost unintelligible whisper, Bertha now speaks in clear tones, with little or none of the German accent of the medium, and very often, no matter where I am placed, comes across the room, and pulls me up with both hands; or, if there is a vacant chair beside me, sits down and begins to talk, apparently not noticing those around her.

At a Thursday afternoon séance, held last spring, she came out very lively; and after a cordial greeting I said, "You are feeling strong to-day; can you not do something to interest us?" She hesitated [44] a moment; then leading me into the middle of the room, looked up laughingly into my face and said, "I will show you how we dress the forms in the cabinet." [A] Stretching out her bare arms, turning them that every one could see that there was nothing in them, she brought the palms of her hands together, rubbing them as if rolling something between them. Very soon there descended from her hands a substance which looked like very white lace.

She continued this until several yards of it lay upon the carpet, and then asked me to kneel down, saying I was too tall for her to work easily. She then took the fabric and made a robe around me, which appeared seamless. On being reminded that there were no sleeves, she took each arm in turn and materialized [45] sleeves. Putting her hand on my head she said, "You have not hair enough," and, rubbing her hand over my head, materialized a wig. This I could not see, but put my hand up and felt of it, and those who were near me said it was in keeping with my own hair and quite an improvement.

Removing the garment, she rolled it into a compact mass, manipulated it a few moments, and it was gone! In materializing and dematerializing this fabric, her arms, which were bare to the shoulders, were stretched out at full length, precluding the possibility of any deception.

Thursday afternoon, Oct. 2, I visited Mrs. Fay's séance with some friends from New Bedford and Cincinnati. When Bertha came out I introduced her to my friends, and asked if she would be kind enough to show them how to make lace. She stepped forward and asked for my [46] handkerchief, which she placed between her hands, manipulating it much after the manner of starching fine fabrics. It was easy to see that the material in her hands was rapidly increasing in volume, and soon the lace began to descend; but instead of being only one piece, there were two, one dark red, and one white, both falling at the same time, each piece about three quarters of a yard wide.

When she had completed it, she held one end, while I took the other and walked across the room, stretching it out to its full length, between three and four yards, so that all could see it; and while it was so held, the controlling spirit shut off the light, showing that the lace was brilliantly illuminated. Bertha then gathered it in, rolled it up and dematerialized it on my shoulder, the light remaining on my coat for nearly a minute after the lace had entirely disappeared.

[47] These things are not new; they are as old as the history of man, and are of common occurrence in India at the present time. They have no possible connection with what is known as sleight-of-hand, or legerdemain. Louis Jacolliot, Chief Justice of Chandenagur, French East Indies, in his able work on Occult Science in India, thus points out the difference:—

"Every European has heard of the extraordinary skill of the Hindoo Fakirs, who are popularly designated under the name of Charmers or Jugglers. They claim to be invested with supernatural powers. Such is the belief of all Asiatic people. When our countrymen are told of their performances, they usually answer, 'Go to the regular magicians; they will show you the same things.'

"To enable the reader to appreciate the grounds of this opinion, it seems necessary to show how the Fakirs operate. The following are facts which no traveller has ventured to contradict:—

[48] "*First.*—They never give public representations in places where the presence of several hundred persons makes it impossible to exercise the proper scrutiny.

"*Second.*—They are accompanied by no assistant, or confederate, as they are usually termed.

"*Third.*—They present themselves in the interior of the house, completely naked, except that they wear, for modesty's sake, a small piece of linen about as large as the hand.

"*Fourth.*—They are not acquainted with goblets, or magic bags, or double-bottomed boxes, or prepared tables, or any of the thousand and one things which our European conjurers find necessary.

"*Fifth.*—They have absolutely nothing in their possession save a small wand of seven knots of bamboo, as big as the handle of a pen-holder, which they hold in their right hand, and a small whistle, about three inches long, which they fasten to one of the locks of their long, straight hair; for, having no clothes, and consequently no pockets, they would otherwise be obliged to hold it constantly in the hand.

"*Sixth.*—They operate, as desired by the person whom they are visiting, either in a sitting [49] or standing posture, or, as the case may require, upon the marble, granite, or stucco pavement of the veranda, or upon the bare ground in the garden.

"*Seventh.*—When they need a subject for the exhibition of magnetic or somnambulistic phenomena, they take any of your servants whom you may designate, no matter whom, and they act with the same facility upon a European in case he is willing to serve.

"*Eighth.*—If they need any article, such as a musical instrument, a cane, a piece of paper, a pencil, etc., they ask you to furnish it.

"*Ninth.*—They will repeat any experiments in your presence as many times as you require, and will submit to any test you may apply.

"*Tenth.*—They never ask any pay, merely accepting, as alms for the temple to which they are attached, whatever you choose to offer them.

"I have travelled through India in every direction for many years, and I can truthfully state that I have never seen a single Fakir who was not willing to comply with any of these conditions.

"It only remains for us to ask whether our more popular magicians would ever consent to dispense with any of their numerous accompaniments, [50] and perform under the same conditions. There is no doubt what the answer would be." Whether the forms or articles exhibited are considered as objects invisibly brought into the room, or created from the atmosphere, they are alike astonishing manifestations of an occult power. It does not simplify or explain these singular phenomena to deny their relation to beings of another life, and refer them to a supposed power in man, the laws of which are unknown to us. We have to deal with them as we would with any of the natural manifestations of life.

To assume that these things are not honest,—that these beings, who come to us claiming to be our friends and relatives, are deceiving us, playing on our credulity,—is to decide the question without evidence.

[A] The control had stated to me, only a few minutes before, that the forms were first materialized and then draped.

[51] CHAPTER IV.
MATERIALIZATION AND DEMATERIALIZATION UNDER TEST CONDITIONS.

At Mrs. Fay's, on Thursday, Oct. 6, 1885, previous to the séance, Mrs. Fay came into the room under the control of "Auntie," and requested that four ladies should be selected by the audience to go with the medium to her dressing-room. The request was complied with, and the ladies returned with Mrs. Fay, still under control, and stated that they had dressed her entirely in dark clothes; that there was not one particle of white fabric about her, except the little collar around her neck. The control then asked me to take a light into the cabinet, and all were requested [52] to examine it and see that there was no possible chance for a confederate, or the concealment of drapery. This was done to the entire satisfaction of all present.

Mrs. Fay was not allowed to leave the room, but, as soon as the audience was seated, went directly into the cabinet. She had not time to take her seat before a form, dressed in white, came out into the room. This was followed by several others similarly dressed.

Then the light was lowered, and a tall female form came out, dressed in brilliantly illuminated garments. A white handkerchief held against this drapery had the appearance of a dark object. This figure walked about the room for a few minutes, and vanished within three feet from where I sat, and at least eight feet from the cabinet.

Then, in the middle of the room, on the [53] carpet, appeared a small light, not larger than the palm of my hand. It gradually grew larger, until it assumed the tall, angular form of "Auntie," the control, who, in her hoarse voice, greeted us with, "Good afternoon, all: I thought I would see what I could do." She then addressed the audience in one of the most forcible speeches I ever listened to, stating her reasons for putting her medium under test conditions, ending by saying that she respected an honest skeptic, but had no patience with those who accept anything without good, substantial evidence.

She returned to the cabinet, and many forms came out and were recognized. Bertha came, and, stretching out her arms at full length, that all could see there was no chance for deception, she materialized between her hands a piece of cambric, about three yards long and one wide, brilliantly illuminated. After all who desired [54] to do so had examined it, she gathered it up, and, passing over to where the light was the strongest, held it up, laughingly remarking that there was enough to make a dress, proceeded to make it up, materializing sleeves, and then put it on and walked round the room. Taking it off, she dematerialized it in the presence of all.

Returning for a moment to the cabinet, she came back, and, kneeling on the floor, with the fingers of the right hand made circular movements on the carpet, with each of which it was plain to be seen that the light was increasing. She continued this until she had materialized another large piece of fabric. This gave great satisfaction to all, except one visitor, who, from some cause, was a little disturbed, and had the kindness to ask me if I had been in the habit of practising sleight-of-hand. His intimate friend, who came with him, had the good fortune to be close to [55] Bertha, and had witnessed all that had occurred. He rose, of his own free will, and stated to the audience that he had been investigating the subject for thirty years, and that this was the most wonderful and convincing thing he had ever seen.

On Thursday, Oct. 13, Mrs. Fay was again put under test conditions. The audience was large, crowding the room and making it so warm as to materially interfere with the manifestations, especially with those spirits who had not been accustomed to materialize. The illuminated forms and drapery were well shown. In the light séance, Bertha came and pulled me up from my chair. She complained of the closeness of the room, saying that she could not do much. She materialized a carnation in my hand, and I called Mr. Whitlock to witness it, whereupon she took both of his hands and made a flower in each.

[56] Emma, one of the controls, soon came out, dressed in a rich white figured satin dress, which all in the front row were allowed to inspect. Mr. Whitlock obtained a pair of scissors, and, with Emma's consent, cut quite a piece out of her dress. The damage seemed to be soon repaired. Mr. Whitlock, in searching for the place where he had cut the piece out, lifted the skirt, which gave Emma a chance to play the coquette, and this created considerable amusement. Mr. Whitlock persevered, and I think is able to state whether he succeeded in spoiling the dress.

A fine-looking form, claiming to be a German chemist, and the control of Dr. Thomas, came out, and magnetized or medicated a tumbler of water, sparks of light flashing freely from his fingers into the water, which was then given to a lady from New Haven, Conn.,— with what effect I cannot say, except that she complained [57] that it tasted bitter. I saw this manifestation for the first time several weeks before, and, I confess, was rather amused with it. While speaking somewhat skeptically of it to a friend who sat beside me, I was surprised when the form came across the room and asked me to take the magnetized water. I had been suffering for some weeks, and, to do the Doctor justice, I must say I was almost entirely relieved.

Mr. Whitlock's father came to him,—a fine, robust form, with a strong individuality that could not well be mistaken. Mr. Whitlock and his wife testified to the likeness. This was followed by the appearance of Dr. J. R. Newton, the widely-known healer, some time deceased. Mr. Whitlock and I went up and greeted him. I shook hands with him, and had time to study his face well: there could be no mistake; it was a wonderful likeness of the Doctor.

[58] The séance, although held under unfavorable circumstances, was full of strong, convincing points. To the above statement, Mr. L. L. Whitlock, Editor of *Facts*, appends the following:—

"At the above-named séance, held on Nov. 13th, the following-named ladies were asked by Mrs. Fay to examine her clothing before she entered the cabinet, viz.:—Mrs. Joseph Harris, of Dorchester, Mass.; Mrs. A. Smith, of Lynn, Mass.; Mrs. J. D. Lillie, Boston; Mrs. M. A. Estee, East Boston; and Mrs. L. L. Whitlock, Providence, R. I.

"They stated that she had nothing white about her person, except a piece of ruche around her neck, worn as a collar. The cabinet was also thoroughly examined by all who desired.

"My father, Rev. Geo. C. Whitlock, LL.D., who passed to the spirit-life about twenty years ago, was very perfectly materialized, so much so that Mrs. Whitlock, who often sees him clairvoyantly, but never saw him in earth-life, recognized him before I saw him, my attention at the moment being attracted by conversation in another direction.

[59] "We will not attempt a description of this séance, as Mr. Brackett's report is substantially what we would have written. Our experience with the dress above mentioned was wonderful, and to us as incomprehensible as was our lace experience at Mrs. Fay's séance at Onset Bay last summer, a description of which we published in the September number of *Facts*.

"One thing is certain: I had in my hand a piece of brocaded white satin, which I know I had cut from the dress of which Mr. Brackett speaks, and that, while I was kneeling before the form, the hole which I had made in the dress did disappear, and that I used my senses, of both sight and feeling, to convince myself of the facts.

"Over sixty forms appeared, most of whom were recognized by friends."

[60] CHAPTER V.
AN UNEXPECTED SÉANCE.

At an interview with Mr. W. C. Tallman, Mr. W. A. Hovey, and Rev. M. J. Savage, the question of obtaining private séances, in the interest of the Committee on Psychical Research, was discussed, and it was considered desirable to make arrangements with Mrs. H. B. Fay for that purpose. I was selected to consult with her, and, if possible, obtain her consent.

As several gentlemen who intended to join us were not present, Mr. Savage was requested to see and inform them of the conditions agreed upon; the result of his [61] interview to be forwarded to me by letter at Mrs. Fay's, on Thursday, before the séance held on that day. These conditions were very simple, and ought to have been satisfactory to any reasonable person. They were the result of the long experience of Mr. Tallman, Mr. Hovey, and myself, made heartily in the interest of the Committee. There was no difference of opinion, Mr. Savage fully endorsing them.

The letter was duly received, and, without stopping to read it, I informed Mrs. Fay that I was ready to talk with her. She replied that she should leave the matter entirely with her control, and if I would lay the letter on the mantel, near the cabinet, Auntie, the control, would probably speak about it. This letter was a long one,—some four pages, written by a member of the Psychological Society, in reply to Mr. Savage. I placed [62] it under a heavy music-box, within a few inches of my head, where I am certain it remained undisturbed until I took it away. Its contents, which reversed the arrangements agreed upon, were not made known to Mrs. Fay until after the decision of her control. As I did not then know what it contained, and in my subsequent interview with Mrs. F. made no allusion to it, Auntie's knowledge of it seemed very remarkable.

As the séance drew near the end, a spirit to whom I am greatly attached called me up to the cabinet; and while I was conversing with her, Auntie's voice broke in, saying, "Mr. Brackett?" I said, "What is it, Auntie?" She replied, "I will see you to-morrow."

I called on Mrs. Fay the next day, and, after talking with her on other matters, and finding that she did not seem disposed to allude to the appointment, I [63] reminded her that I came on business. She asked, "What is it?" I replied that Auntie had requested me to meet her. She rose without a moment's hesitation, saying, "We will go to the cabinet." This was a surprise to me, for I fully expected that Auntie would take control of her medium, and talk to me through her, as she had often done before.

As Mrs. Fay stepped behind the curtain, Auntie came out, fully materialized, greeting me cordially, shaking hands with me, and expressing pleasure at meeting me; then, in a clear and forcible manner, discussed the question of the proposed séance, going freely into detail, showing conclusively that she understood both sides, and closed by saying that she did not propose to submit her medium to such conditions as were required by the letter, at the same time expressing a willingness to do all she could for Mr. Savage [64] personally. Bidding me Good-bye, she dematerialized directly in front of me, so near that I could have laid my hand upon her as she went down. The curtains were apart, and I could see Mrs. Fay standing just beside the cabinet; but, in order to make me more certain, if possible, of that fact, she reached out her right hand, which I took in my left, preventing the curtains from closing; and while thus standing, no less than six fully materialized forms came out and greeted me.

During all this time Mrs. Fay may have been under partial control, but was not entranced, and talked freely with me about the forms, often describing them before they were visible to me.

These forms were substantial, varying in height and shape, and distinct from each other. Most of them conversed freely, showing quite as much individuality and intelligence as some of my [65] acquaintances to whom forms sometimes appear,—persons who think they are wise in treating these forms with coldness and distrust, all of which is reflected back to them.

It is easy to understand why such persons are disappointed in what comes to them; but it is not easy to understand how any intelligent investigator, who has given the subject any considerable attention, should come to the conclusion that the forms are automatons, and that our friends from the other side never take possession, or control them, as they would a trance-medium; that they are merely effigies, [B] or lay figures, built up to mock us, and play with the most sacred feelings of our natures; and, what is more diabolical, that our spirit-friends are near by, enjoying the base deception! If this view is correct, what a fearful amount of lying there must be in every séance! Such a conclusion would be impossible from what passed before me at this sitting.

[66] As I gazed with delight upon this sudden and unexpected manifestation, bathed in a mellow light which made all the surroundings perfectly visible, I could not help feeling a regret that my Psychical friends had shut themselves out from such evidence by requiring arrangements to which no intelligent control would submit. Here, under strictly test conditions, which precluded any possible doubt, was crowded into a small space just the information which I am sure that some of them are honestly endeavoring to obtain.

[67] These things may be nothing but a mere phantasy of the mind; what is claimed as exact science, a humbug; and life itself only a delusion; but those whose lives are rounded into a full consciousness of an individual existence may prefer to consider them in a different light. The same perception which enables us to recognize one must be conceded to the other.

If, in the search after facts relating to the more subtle forms of life, the testimonies of thousands of honest and intelligent persons are to be disregarded, we might as well abolish our courts. Judge, jury, and witness become nothing but ridiculous actors in a farce played in the name of Justice.

[B] In an essay written by "Shadows," intended to enlighten the public on this subject, he puts forth the theory of effigies. In the same article he relates a séance with the Berry Sisters, in which he says that "a young female spirit came to him." The word spirit must have been a slip of the pen; he should have said, a young female effigy. It was possibly in anticipation of his theory that the young effigy called him "father!"

[68] CHAPTER VI.
SÉANCE WITH MRS. CARRIE M. SAWYER.

Among the strong points in evidence of the genuineness of these manifestations are the marked individuality and constant variations that appear. The séances with the same medium will be found to differ widely; no two of them are exactly alike. Sometimes they will be exceedingly good, and at other times almost an entire failure. If they were in any way due to confederates, or to personation by the medium, such variations would not be likely to occur.

Again, the séances with one medium differ essentially from those with another; [69] so much so that each medium may be said to have a phase of mediumship distinct in itself. The forms may appear quite different in outward shape, when coming through one medium from what they do in coming through another. The mental characteristics will, however, as I have found, be retained in both instances. This has often led to confusion and distrust with those who visit different séances. The tendency is very strong to give precedence to mere outward appearance, without reference to character.

In no case is the old adage, "A little learning is a dangerous thing," more applicable than to the study of this subject. The shallow investigators, the touch-and-go people, will, in most cases, find themselves left in bewilderment and doubt. These things are not to be settled by witnessing one or two séances. Nor is the character of the manifestations, as expressed [70] through any medium, to be determined without considerable experience.

From statements, and especially from the impression I received on my first interview with Mrs. Sawyer, I was led to expect much from her séance. My first séance with her was a disappointment, there being nothing except the delightful interview with little Maud, one of the "cabinet spirits," [C] to attract the attention of any one familiar with these things. It is due her to say, in explanation, that it was her first séance in Boston, and held under unfavorable conditions.

On the 11th of August, I again visited her séance, in company with Mrs. Fay. The day was very hot, with a close, moist atmosphere, rendering the séance-room very uncomfortable. The only wonder was that, under such conditions, there [71] could have been any manifestations whatever. I was seated on one side of Mrs. Fay, and a friend of hers on the other. This trio, so to speak, drew the fire of the whole séance; the only strong and decided manifestations appearing on that side of the circle.

Auntie, Mrs. Fay's control, stood behind us, invisible to all except her medium, occasionally making remarks in her hoarse, unmistakable voice. Coming, as the voice did, out of space, with no organized being in sight to produce it, the effect was at times startling.

A very sprightly spirit came briskly up to Mrs. Fay, extending her hands, and leading her up to the cabinet, where they conversed for some time. This was followed by what claimed to be Bertha. She came very lively, greeting me cordially. The form was very like, and the expression of character assuring, but, [72] owing to the unusually poor light and hasty interview, I prefer to withhold conclusions for the present. More decided in its character was another spirit that followed soon after. There was a centre-table between me and the cabinet. This spirit, instead of coming into the middle of the room, passed to the left, moving the table out, and coming directly to me. This brought her more in the light, where I had a better opportunity of seeing her. Both of these spirits appeared to be the exact counterparts of those who had come to me so often at Mrs. Fay's, but who at other places exhibited a great deal of variation. Was the close resemblance due to the fact that Mrs. Fay was sitting by my side? The question is an interesting one, suggesting further experience.

It may be well to state here that every opportunity was granted for examining the cabinet, which I did to my entire satisfaction. [73] I also obtained from the builder a certified statement that it was constructed of kiln-dried lumber, tongued and grooved, nailed, screwed, and glued together in such a way as to render it impossible to remove the boards, or for a confederate to enter it except through the door in the audience-room, in the presence of the visitors. All were permitted to inspect it before the medium took her seat. There could be no question but that the cabinet and its surroundings were above suspicion. This left me free to study the manifestations purely as materializations, or personations by the medium. I know that the forms that came to me were distinct individual beings, and in no instance was I able to discover any indications that would lead me to suppose that the medium personated any of the forms.

At the next séance which I visited, [74] on Sept. 15, the weather was again oppressive, so much so that the séance would have been abandoned had it not been that some of the visitors, who had come from another State, were unwilling to give it up. Notwithstanding the excessive heat, the séance proved a very interesting one.

While little Maud was standing at the curtain talking, there was a remarkable show of hands and arms above her head. Sometimes six of them would be moving back and forth outside the curtain at once. About eight feet from the cabinet, and directly in front of me, so near that I could have touched it without moving from my seat, appeared a very delicate little hand and arm. Like a bird that hovers around some object that it dare not approach too closely, this hand and arm dallied and played before me for several minutes, visible to all present. [75] On the left side of the room, more than six feet from the cabinet door, a form materialized in full view, and came forward and shook hands with a lady on my right.

While engrossed in these things, I had almost forgotten that my principal object in being there was to study the form of Bertha as compared with her appearance at other places. I was aroused from my meditations by an involuntary shock that almost always warns me of what is coming. Turning quickly around, I saw what appeared to be Bertha, gliding from the cabinet. She passed rapidly to the left side of the room, moving the centre-table and coming directly to me. Throwing her arms around my neck, she greeted me with, "I love you," and then, with a frightened expression and half hysterical laugh, she retreated to the cabinet. This was totally unlike Bertha, who, in her perfectly confiding and childlike bearing [76] toward me, never felt it necessary to express her feelings in any such bold declaration. Knowing that there are phantoms that can take on almost any form they choose, the outward resemblance of these beings has no weight with me, in the absence of mental characteristics.

At a séance held by Mrs. Sawyer, Sept. 29, there were present twenty-five persons, most of whom received more or less attention from the spirits. Little Maud was very lively and full of witty, playful remarks. Near the close of the séance, she asked me to come into the cabinet and try to quiet the medium, who was exhausted in consequence of having watched with a sick friend the previous night. On entering the cabinet, I found that Mrs. Sawyer was not entranced, and took hold of both her hands, endeavoring to give her all the mesmeric strength I could.

[77] While thus situated, conversing

freely with the medium and little Maud (who was evidently pleased to have me there), a spirit materialized and went out among the audience. After it returned, another materialized, and taking my left hand while Mrs. Sawyer held my right, we all three walked out into the room, some distance from the cabinet, in full view of all present. This was a new experience for me. To suppose that the twenty-five honest, intelligent persons who witnessed this were deceived, or that the appearance of the form was due to a confederate, is simply absurd. I know it materialized in the cabinet, within reach of where I sat.

What was claimed by the manager to be Bertha came out, and I gave her a test to be used by her at another séance.

In following the rôle of strict investigation, and in honestly relating what has come to me at these séances, I am forced [78] to state that the form that appeared on this occasion was not Bertha, and that there was, as subsequent events proved, an attempt to deceive me. Mrs. Sawyer is a gentlewoman and a strong medium, but she is surrounded by a coarse magnetism, the baleful influence of which she seems powerless to resist.

[C] This term is applied to spirits who appear to be constant attendants or assistants in the cabinets of mediums for materialization.

[79] CHAPTER VII.
SÉANCES WITH MRS. FAIRCHILD.

The mediumship of Mrs. Fairchild differs from that of others inasmuch as she stands outside of the cabinet, under the influence of one of her controls, managing the séance with great skill and judgment, thus eliminating from her séances all chance of transfiguration or personation by the medium, forcing the skeptic or investigator to the conclusion that the forms are either genuine materializations or confederates.

The position of her cabinet, placed as it is between two rooms, is certainly open to criticism. A thorough examination of [80] it, however, revealed no possible chance for the concealment of draperies or the entrance of a confederate.

In order to meet the objections which have been made to this arrangement, she has drawn a light curtain across the corner of the room. Backed as it is by solid walls, the forms that come from this temporary cabinet cannot be confederates, and the skeptic may answer as best he can the question, What are they?

This cabinet, however, is only used occasionally, and the average visitor sees only what comes from the main cabinet. If this temporary arrangement is so successful, and I know it is, there is some force in the objection made against using the other. Every medium is in justice bound to give to visitors the best conditions possible. Mr. Whitlock thus describes séances held with Mrs. Fairchild, Sept. 12 and 19:—

[81] "The medium was controlled in a few moments by 'Cadaleene,' a very interesting spirit, who managed the séance with perfect nonchalance, selecting with ease and correctness the persons whom the spirits desired to come to the cabinet, thereby fulfilling the double office, with Mrs. Fairchild, of medium and manager.

"During this séance the medium was outside, and in view of the audience, except on one or two occasions, when she went into the cabinet for a moment; and at the last, when her control, Cadaleene, who had promised to materialize, came out so perfect in action and voice that I shall never forget her grateful attentions as she knelt at my side. Time after time more than one form was out of the cabinet at the same moment, and in one case five persons, including a child.

"One of the most convincing proofs of materialization was the following: A lady, whom we understood to be a relative of Col. Bailey, called him up to the cabinet and kissed him; and while he was standing with both arms around her, talking, she dematerialized. This occurred fully three feet from the cabinet, in sight of the audience, a dozen of whom must [82] have been within six feet of the form, and some of them as near the cabinet.

"The following Saturday, Sept. 19, we again attended her afternoon séance. At this séance we found Mrs. Isabella Beecher Hooker, of Hartford, Conn.; Mr. Thomas Hazard, of Providence, R. I.; Mr. John Wetherbee, of Boston, and many other well known persons, were present.

"What we have already written in reference to Cadaleene and her control of the medium, is equally applicable to this séance; also the expressions of confidence in reference to the cabinet. I had expressed to a friend, whom I met in the office of the *Banner of Light*, that while, to the best of my knowledge, after an examination, I believed Mrs. Fairchild's cabinet to be all right, still I would like to see the same results in a cabinet made by hanging a curtain across the corner of the room. Judge of my surprise when, after the séance had commenced, Cadaleene said, 'Mr. Facts-man, I heard what you told the brave, and you see we have the curtain across the corner, to show you what we can do.'

"The séance continued in the regular cabinet, [83] as usual, for about an hour and a half. The light was good, and many spirits manifested their presence, among which the following interesting experience occurred: A gentleman, who does not choose to have his name mentioned, had a communication the day before from a spirit-friend, in writing, through his own hand, promising to materialize at this séance. He told me that this spirit had not only fulfilled this promise, but had told him things that no other person knew but himself, and that he recognized her fully.

"Then came the crowning glory of the séance. The control, Cadaleene, still holding the medium, directed that the gas be lit and the hall door opened. She then closed the sliding door in front of the cabinet, and fastened back the curtains which hung over it to form the front of the regular cabinet when in use, so that all might know if it was opened.

"The audience was then seated facing the corner where the curtains had been hung for a temporary cabinet, some near and in front of the door just mentioned, which could be seen by all present. The medium, still under control, passed behind the curtain, but came out in [84] a moment, followed almost immediately by a form dressed entirely in white. After this form returned to the cabinet, two others came out,—one a lady, the other a gentleman,—and it was said a third was seen in the cabinet.

"All this time the medium was controlled by Cadaleene, who was finding the friends of the spirits with remarkable dexterity. Several others followed, and we might give names and personal experiences, but feel that our readers will appreciate most these special points of interest."

Mrs. Isabella Beecher Hooker, Mr. Thomas Hazard, and Mr. John Wetherbee have given graphic descriptions of these séances.

On Tuesday, Oct. 13, in company with William D. Brewer, I attended a private séance with Mrs. Fairchild. I examined the cabinet without being able to discover anything that would lead me to suppose that there was any chance for a confederate to be used. The séance lasted [85] about two hours, during which time scarcely a minute passed that there were not forms out in the room, either to Mr. Brewer or myself; sometimes three or four at once. More than half the time the extemporized cabinet in the corner of the room was used. There appeared to be no difference between the workings of the two; the manifestations came as freely from one as from the other.

As I examined the walls and everything connected with the temporary cabinet, I have no hesitation in saying that the forms that came from or appeared in it were materialized beings. I was in this cabinet several times during the séance, often with two forms at the same time. Once I sat between them, an arm around each, satisfying myself of their objective reality as well as if I had been walking with them outside in the room. While thus holding them, the one encircled by my left arm, [86] and whose right arm was around my neck, instantly disappeared, without the slightest indication of any movement;—she was there, and she was not there. Still holding the one encircled by my right arm, I rose and with my left hand drew the curtain aside, so that I could see everything behind it. There was not the faintest trace of the beautiful being that, a moment before, I had so firmly held, and with whom I had been talking.

Similar things have occurred to me in various ways, so often that they produce no surprise, only an earnest desire to discover how or where the forms go, or possibly gain some knowledge of the laws governing these strange phenomena.

The force at Mrs. Fairchild's séances is mainly expended in materialization, and for that reason they are valuable to skeptics; but to the experienced investigator they offer nothing new. Many of the [87] forms come heavily veiled, and there is an absence of that social and mental character which is ever the surest evidence of recognition.

[88] CHAPTER VIII.
SÉANCE WITH MISS HELEN BEERY AT ONSET.

"Spirits are never finely touched
But to fine issues; nor Nature never lends
The smallest scruple of her excellence,
But, like a thrifty goddess, she determines
Herself the glory of the creditor,
Both thanks and use."

At one of Miss Helen Berry's séances at Onset in the summer of 1885, there came a young female spirit, apparently about sixteen years old. She took me by both hands and led me up to the cabinet, where she greeted me very warmly. As she could bear more light than most of the forms, I had no difficulty in studying her face and figure. She was a little below the average height, lithe and graceful in all her movements. A cloud of [89] dark golden hair drifted around her neck and shoulders, falling far below her waist. Her dress was pure white, of a rich fabric, so thin that it revealed a form beautiful as the finest Greek statue. She appeared more like a dream of ideal life, than a creature who had ever walked the earth.

There are moments of exultation in the life of every artist, when his soul reaches out to visions of great beauty. No canvas or marble can record these visions. In his associations with the world, he may, at times, catch glimpses that remind him of what he has seen, but nowhere does he realize, as a whole, the perfection of those forms that have allured him from his ordinary surroundings.

Was this charming creature one of those beings who had haunted my dreams?—who, in the still hours of the night, had sometimes dispelled the darkness by the glow of her presence?

[90] If I hesitated a moment in recognizing her, it was because she had never before appeared clothed in so beautiful a form, or if so I had failed to appreciate it. Perhaps it was due, in part, to the negative condition I was in, which allowed a freer and more perfect development, undisturbed by any mental action on my part; and this idea is strengthened by the fact that, in all my connection with these séances, what I most desired to obtain seldom came until after I had become more or less indifferent about it. As I stood beside this form, I passed my fingers through her long silken tresses, and put my hand upon her finely formed head. As she laid her face to mine, she said in the most earnest yet tender tones, "You did not think I would come." This was true; tired with my journey and the sultry heat, I was indifferent to taking an active part in the séance. I was, however, [91] in a listless way, interested in what came to others, and had given up expecting that anything would come to me; and yet, had I reflected for a moment, I should have known that at any true séance, where I was present and the conditions favorable, it would have been hardly possible for her to keep away. The consciousness of her presence at other times than in the séance-room is no uncommon occurrence with me.

In the séance-room, where she comes so strong and substantial, I have often put forth little playful, but somewhat provocative remarks, in order to draw out, as far as possible, an expression of her character. Sometimes these things excited her, but never, except for the moment, disturbed the harmony between us.

At this interview I was not in a condition of mind likely to attract spirits, whether in or out of the flesh. In the [92] course of conversation, I dropped a remark that disturbed her. She grasped my hand nervously, her chest rose and fell with increased respiration, and without making any reply she retreated to the cabinet.

Thinking it possible that I might have displeased her, and that she would not return, I went to my seat. A moment afterward, I was surprised by her rushing out and kneeling down in front of me. Throwing her bare arms around my neck and pulling my head down to her, that others might not listen to what was said, she poured forth, in the most earnest and impassioned strain, her thoughts; talking as only a woman can talk under the highest inspiration.

I had long since abandoned all doubts of the existence of these beings, and had been, in a quiet and affectionate way, studying the different phases of character [93] manifested by them. Like many others who have investigated this subject, I had met with things which I could not understand or harmonize with my experience. This was leading me to conclusions that I intuitively felt were not true, and yet I could not extricate myself from the network of apparent evidence that surrounded me.

That she understood my mental condition, was evinced by the fact that her whole force and energy were directed to this one subject. Her form trembled and vibrated with emotion as she uttered sentence after sentence in clear explanation of what had perplexed me. Raising her head, and tossing back her long hair, she grasped both my hands, and, with a face beaming with light, said:

"It seems strange to you, but what can I do? We are subject to conditions; and if I come at all, it must be in harmony [94] with them. There are spheres and circles we cannot penetrate, if the controlling influence is against us. We are still human, still yearning for affection,—that love which is the silken cord that binds us all. What would you not do to reach those dear to your heart? You understand me now."

There was a remarkably childlike simplicity in the way she unburdened her mind, giving free expression to her feelings, bearing me mentally along with her, until I was lost to everything else. That is all. There are thoughts and feelings which no language can express. Like the silvery notes of a sweet song that echo in the distance, they revel in their freedom from restraint, and forever elude our grasp.

I know the breath that fans my cheek,
The thoughts, the words I cannot speak,
The arms that round me twine.[95]
What need of words when thoughts are told
In light that gleams like burnished gold,
With pulse that throbs to mine?

Never before had I listened to such eloquence. Every word, with its rich intonation, is indelibly stamped upon my memory, and I regret that, for personal reasons, it cannot be recorded here.

Exhausted by her long effort, as she rose and led me to the cabinet, I noticed that her form was rapidly changing. Suddenly, like the extinguishing of a light, she passed into that invisible space whence she came.

There were no "test conditions" here; and there might have been a dozen confederates, for aught I can prove. It is barely possible that this delightful being belonged on this side of life; but whether on this side or the other, in the fulness of my artistic nature, I thanked God that such beauty could exist anywhere. The [96] evidence of truthfulness in what came to me at this séance rests on something stronger than barred windows and locked doors;—it was in the complete embodiment of the character, both mentally and physically.

The séance closed, and I returned to Glen Cove by the road that skirts the shore. The south wind played with the blue waters of the bay, throwing up myriads of little waves that danced in the moonlight. As I stood gazing upon the sea, baring my feverish brow to the cooling breeze, I felt that my whole nature was flowing out into a vast circle of being. Thoughts, words, feelings, all blended with the mellow light which flooded the scene. If I was not supremely happy, it was not from lack of harmony with everything around me.

There is ever a tinge of sadness in the background of life. With the beauty of [97] the waves comes the low moan as they break upon the shore. With the warmth of friendship, comes the pain of parting, and, sadder still, that relentless fate that hurries us from those we love into the dim, uncertain future. The sands of life are golden only where thought diffuses itself without shadows, and the light that charms us flows from the object of our affections.

It was late, and I retired for the night—closed my eyes, but not to sleep. The walls of my room disappeared, and my vision swept over an undefined and illimitable space. Before me like a mist, but perfectly outlined, glided the beautiful being who only a few minutes before had come so close to me. Soon she was joined by others, lightly drifting, floating through the air.

As round the mountain's craggy steep
The trailing vapors curve and sweep,
So, hand in hand and side by side,
Through space unmeasured, soft they glide.[98]
Now there, now here—so far, so near—
With <u>outstretched</u> arms they beckoned me,
And, like the murmur of the sea,
Their voices broke upon my ear.

As they passed near me, a hand was laid upon my face; I started, sprang up, looked around; there was no one in the room. All was still save the low surging of the tide that swept the beach below.

[99] CHAPTER IX.
SÉANCE AT THE BERRY SISTERS' IN BOSTON.

In looking over my notes, my attention is strongly drawn to the many remarkable things I have witnessed at the Berry Sisters'. As I have given a drawing of Mrs. Fay's cabinet, and its surroundings, which I know to be honest, I give a carefully drawn plan of the séance-room here (see next page). It will be seen that this is one of the most simple and truthful arrangements possible, and the thanks of every investigator are due to the able manager and controls for placing the cabinet in a way that every one can see at a glance that a confederate is out of the question. I have attended several séances at this place since this arrangement has been adopted; and, so far from injuring the manifestations, they are, if anything, improved. [100]

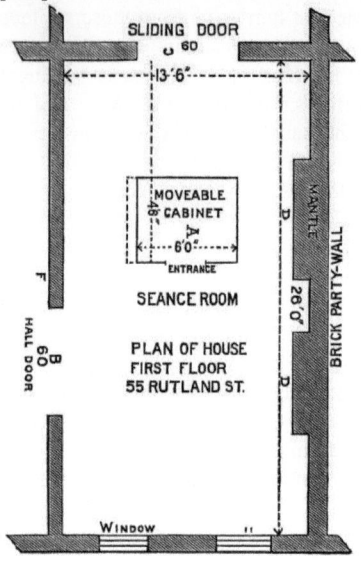

Diagram of the Misses Berry's Séance-Room.

[101] At these séances, when I have been present, Bertha has materialized outside of the cabinet, more than three feet from it, and at least six feet from the entrance, and on one occasion so close to me that she brushed me with her garments as she rose.

On Saturday, Nov. 7, 1885, I attended in company with my wife and little daughter—Mrs. A. E. Newton, of Arlington, also making one of the party. Although the atmosphere was unfavorable, the manifestations were good, there often being two forms out at once, talking with their friends. My seat was on the right, facing the cabinet, and very near to it. Before the séance commenced, by the request of Mr. Albro, the manager, I locked the door [102] at the farther end of the room; and when this was done, he offered me the privilege of sitting beside it. I declined, preferring to take part in the séance.

I will state, however, for the benefit of those who have any doubt about this arrangement, that the seat I occupied commanded a full view of this door, and that I unlocked it after the séance, and can state positively that it was impossible for the door to have been opened without my knowing it. Again, the cabinet is so constructed that if a confederate had entered, he would have been obliged to go around to the front, in full view of the audience, before he could have passed into the cabinet. Those persons whose fertile brains are always leading them into absurd conclusions, will have to seek for some other explanation than that of a confederate here.

In the course of the séance, I had warning of Bertha's presence, and requested [103] Mrs. Newton, who sat beside me, to watch the left-hand corner, near the cabinet. In a few minutes there appeared a soft light on the carpet, near the wall, and almost instantly Bertha came up in full view of all.

Springing forward and taking my little daughter by both hands, she came briskly across the room to where I sat. After our usual greeting, I introduced her to Mrs. Newton, who detained her for some time, my wife coming forward and joining in the conversation. I have described this beautiful spirit so fully in the preceding chapter that it is unnecessary to repeat it here.

Many persons will find it desirable to make themselves familiar with the different phases of materialization as expressed through different mediums; but nowhere else will they find more strength combined with delicacy and refinement, as shown [104] both in the beauty of the forms and their affectionate bearing. Neither in the controls, the forms, nor the surroundings, is there anything here to offend the most fastidious taste. These séances appear to have advanced beyond the mere fact of materialization, offering to those whose magnetic relations are in accord with conditions, a more attractive expression of social and mental character than is frequently met with. As Mrs. Newton seemed quite interested in Bertha, I felt desirous to know what impression was made upon one so well prepared to form a just opinion on such matters. To my expressed wish she kindly responded with the following statement:—

" Arlington, Mass., Nov. 11, 1885.

" My Dear Mr. Brackett,—

"In accordance with your request that I would give you my observations and impressions in regard to the materialized apparition claiming [105] to be your spirit-niece, Bertha, I will state that I think her the most intelligent and sprightly re-embodiment of a spirit that I ever saw,—and I have seen a great many within the last ten years. At all events, I am confident no one who sees her can imagine her to be either a made-up figure, a lifeless effigy, or the medium in disguise.

"At Mrs. Fay's séance, where I first saw her, she showed, on meeting you, that spiritual illumination in the face which joy and gladness give to us when we meet those we love, after an absence. She had also those fine intonations of the voice that can spring only from the affections. Can it be, said I to myself, that this beautiful girl, so charming and graceful, so full of life and intelligence, is truly a spirit? Just as the thought had formed itself in my mind, she had turned toward the cabinet and vanished before the curtain. But hardly a minute had elapsed before she sprang out again from the cabinet, like a new-born seraph, and, opening her hands before all the company present, her arms being entirely bare to the shoulder, she extended them above her head, began to manipulate something apparently in the air, and soon handed [106] me a most exquisite rose, with the moisture oozing from the stem where it had apparently been twisted off from the stock.

"When at Miss Helen Berry's séance, a few days later, I had the assurance made doubly sure that she was not a being of earth, by seeing, about three feet from the cabinet, a small, white, cloud-like substance expand until it was four or five feet high, when suddenly from it the full, round, sylph-like form of Bertha stepped forward. Seeing her little cousin and namesake (Bertha Brackett, nine years old), she took both the child's hands in hers, drew her from her chair, and, after greeting her affectionately, led her playfully across the room to where we were sitting. There I studied every lineament of her face. Her hair had all the warmth and glossiness of that of a healthy girl of eighteen. She said to me, 'Don't you think I am very strong to-day?' and, putting both hands in mine, allowed me to caress and converse with her freely. 'Do you remember you materialized a rose for me last week?' I asked. 'Yes,' she replied, 'and you have it now at home.' This was true.

"Mrs. Brackett called my attention to the length and beauty of Bertha's hair, and asked [107] her if she could not make it longer if she wished to. 'Yes,' she laughingly replied; 'but it will grow shorter if I don't get to the cabinet soon!' and, with a graceful adieu, she tripped across the room, leading her little cousin into the cabinet with her, where she dematerialized in the child's presence.

"Since witnessing the foregoing, I have re-read your account of the séance with Miss Berry at Onset, and I feel quite safe in saying your description of Bertha is not overdrawn. She certainly exhibits an individuality intensely human, and yet not of ordinary flesh-and-blood, as shown by her sudden appearance and disappearance. She proves beyond a doubt that, given the same conditions and opportunities to other spirits that you have afforded her, they may come with the same fulness of life and strength.

"I cannot refrain from expressing the hope that some of the members of the Seybert Commission will come to Boston and study Bertha—see her materialize three feet from the cabinet, as we did—hear her converse intelligently—see the divinely moulded form—and then witness, as we did, her sudden change to another sphere of being, doubtless to engage in pleasant [108] duties among that deathless throng who are ever learning, and who will unfold to us, if we will become receptive, the laws of entrancement and of materialization. It seems scarcely possible that these gentlemen would fail to be convinced that 'there are more things in heaven and earth than are dreamed of' in materialistic 'philosophy.'

"Very truly yours,
S. J. Newton ."

[109] CHAPTER X. MATERIALIZED FORMS— HOW SHALL WE MEET THEM?

Years ago I had a friend who was generous to a fault. He freely gave wherever he thought there was need. With all his liberality, he was singularly successful in business, and when he passed to the other life left a large fortune, which was mainly distributed to charitable institutions.

Walking with him one day, we passed some beggars sitting on the sidewalk,—pitiful specimens of humanity, with large placards in front of them, detailing the misfortunes that had befallen them. One, not over thirty years old, had lost a leg in the battle of Waterloo; another had lost [110] his eyes by an eruption of Vesuvius which must have occurred twenty years before he was born. The cards must have been heirlooms, handed down at least one generation. These little discrepancies apparently made no impression on my friend, who emptied his pockets of his spare change, giving something to each of them. As we passed on, I said to him, "Do you know that these poor fellows were up before the police court a few days ago for being engaged in a drunken brawl?" I shall never forget the expression of his face as he turned to me and said, "It is my duty as well as my pleasure to give; the responsibility of using it is theirs, not mine."

Many years had come and gone, and the memory of my friend had almost faded from my mind. I was engaged in studying materialization. As my custom is to take one thing at a time, I did not [111] trouble myself about the quality. I did not even propose to myself what I might do afterward; but did propose, if there was any truth in it, to so clearly demonstrate it that no doubts should come up as a disturbing element in any subsequent investigations I might make.

When I had finished my investigations on this point, I found that I stood on the shore of a boundless sea of speculation and uncertainty. I could not help asking myself the question, "What are these forms that, for a few minutes only, clothe themselves in objective reality, bearing the semblance of my friends, blended with the likeness of the medium? Are these my father, my mother, my wife, my brother? Is this the rollicking boy who made the hills echo with his laughter, now whispering in my ear so low that I can scarcely hear him?"

In the midst of this perplexity, this [112] whirl of unanswered questions, the voice of my old friend came to me: "Don't stare these sensitive beings out of countenance, but give to them all that you can of your better nature, and you shall have your reward. If there is a possibility of mistake as to identity, if you are in any way deceived, the responsibility is theirs, not yours. In all true séances, if the forms are not what they are supposed to be, they are, at least, beings from another life, seeking strength and comfort from association with you, else they would not come. Let not a shadow of doubt or distrust bar their approach. Have no awe, no reserve, no fear as to what they are, and they will blend into your soul, become a part of your life. In the true relations which you hold to them will be the fulness of what they bring to you."

With a nature naturally skeptical, and a mind long trained to a close comparison [113] of objects, it was not easy to accept this advice. What, then, was to be done? It was plain that I must move on, or abandon all that I had so successfully demonstrated.

I could not launch out into the endless speculation of "psychical research;" I had not time for that; so I decided to follow the course which had been suggested to me. I would lay aside all reserve, and greet these forms as dear departed friends, who had come from afar, and had struggled hard to reach me.

From that moment the forms, which

had seemed to lack vitality, became animated with marvellous strength. They sprang forward to greet me; tender arms were clasped around me; forms that had been almost dumb during my investigations now talked freely; faces that had worn more the character of a mask than of real life now glowed with beauty. What [114] claimed to be my niece, ever pleasant and earnest in aiding me to obtain the knowledge I was seeking, overwhelmed me with demonstrations of regard. Throwing her arms around me, and laying her head upon my shoulder, she looked up and said, "Now we can all come so near you!" Her wonderful spontaneity of character at once asserted itself, and has ever since been the delight of all who have come in contact with her.

My association with these forms is of the most simple character; it is that of children with each other: we realize the full force of the Master's words, "Except ye become as little children, ye shall not enter the kingdom of heaven." Science may wrangle over the supposed movements of molecules and atoms, and the correlation of forces; may dissect the bird to find its song; but love alone shall set the boundaries of knowledge. The key [115] that unlocks the glories of another life is pure affection, simple and confiding as that which prompts the child to throw its arms around its mother's neck.

To those who pride themselves upon their intellectual attainments, this may seem to be a surrender of the exercise of what they call the higher faculties. So far from this being the case, I can truly say that until I adopted this course, sincerely and without reservation, I learned nothing about these things. Instead of clouding my reason and judgment, it opened my mind to a clearer and more intelligent perception of what was passing before me. That spirit of gentleness, of loving kindness, which, more than anything else, crowns with eternal beauty the teachings of the Christ, should find its full expression in our association with these beings. [116]

[117] Part II.
OPINIONS AND THEORIES.

[118]
[119] The credulous have their weak points, but the belief of unbelievers surpasses all credulity.

There is no position a man can assume so weak as that of extreme skepticism in the face of fair evidence. [120] [121] Heat, light, electricity, and force are common things. We accept them as matters of everyday life; our familiarity with them prevents surprise. In our attempts to discover or learn what they are we have utterly failed. All that we have found is how they act under certain conditions. They are the elements necessary to the existence of physical life, and by cultivating their acquaintance we have made friends with them. They walk beside us, lending a helping hand in everything; still they are our masters—we know them not. For the moment we comprehend a thing we are greater than the thing we comprehend: it is behind us, not in front.

Those who are seeking to know how these spirit-forms are created will seek in vain, for there is no language by which the process can be conveyed to our understanding. When it is said that they come out of invisible space, and depart in the same way, all is said that can be in explanation of their advent among us. [122]

[123] OPINIONS AND THEORIES.

CHAPTER I.
A GLANCE BEHIND THE CURTAIN.

The nature of man is, to a certain extent, dual. The brain is divided into two parts; there are two sets of nerves crossing each other, so that an injury received on the left side of the brain affects the right side of the body, and *vice versa*. While the duplicated organs are capable of separate action, anatomically suggesting two distinct beings, they are united so as to form a complete union of both. There is, however, a preponderance of brain or will-force [124] in the left side of the head, giving a more complete control over the right side of the body, and, in some instances, a manifestation of character, which would indicate that each side of the brain might act in alternation, and somewhat independently of the other.

The force which the brain exerts over its own organism and that of others is not understood. Could it be explained, all the phenomena of the material and spiritual would, probably, lie within reach. A person with a strong will may possess a magnetic power enabling him to throw another, of a peculiar temperament, into a trance, in which that person is physically insensible to everything except what comes through the sensibility of the magnetizer.

The material bodies are brought *en rapport* with each other, or under the law of individual control, and the magnetizer [125] can direct the physical movements of the other very much as he would his own, leaving the spirit of the entranced person free to act, for the time being, independently of its own body. If it has the strength or power to control other sensitives, it may manifest itself in remote places, either clairvoyantly or by materialization more or less tangible. It can, however, do this much more perfectly in close proximity to its own body. Such a materialization is a counterpart of the entranced person; is, in fact, the spirit of that person clothed in a body not strictly its own, but composed of material largely drawn from it. The existence of this phenomenon has been more or less known through all ages, and is probably the origin of that mythical story of the creation of woman, where the Lord is said to have caused a deep sleep to fall upon Adam.

[126] Among all nations, traditions of what is known as "the double" exist. Though often classed as a vulgar superstition, it nevertheless finds expression in the works of some of the best intellects. It plays an important part in the progress and development of all physical séances, since it is the first indication of true materialization. Furthermore, the substance composing this counterpart is, to a certain extent, the nucleus around which all spirits materializing are developed or clothed.

The form appears to issue from the

left side, but in reality it comes from the whole circumference of the body, in a rapidly-moving luminous vapor, which quickly consolidates into a separate individualized form, complete in its organization, and capable, for the time, of physical and mental action. Such manifestations are what is understood to be the production [127] of living forms by means of living matter given off from the body of the medium. The process is more or less affected by the surroundings, and is ever the result of more intelligent beings coöperating with the spirit of the entranced person.

The spirit occupying this temporary body can, when proper relations have been established with it, surrender it into the control of other spirits, the same as it surrendered its other body into the control of the magnetizer, and from its peculiar structure they can contract, expand, or change it to suit his or her requirements. So long as it remains in the possession of the spirit of the entranced person, the likeness to it is maintained; but the moment it passes into the possession of another, the resemblance will depend entirely upon the strength of the control, and the knowledge the spirit has in shaping the form like to that [128] borne in earth-life. From these conditions materialization may broaden into more complex forms, always depending upon the currents of magnetic thought, and that central will-force that sweeps into its vortex all atoms necessary to its use.

Until the spirits acquire more than ordinary strength by frequent manifestations, or by favorable surroundings, this will probably be found to be the usual way in which they make themselves visible to us. These conditions necessitate more or less resemblance to the medium, both in form and intonations of voice.

I have seen hundreds and thousands of materialized forms; have seen, in a few instances, personation, where the medium was taken possession of, brought out, and controlled as in trance-mediumship; I have seen what appeared to be the double of the medium, so thoroughly like, that I [129] should have testified that it was the medium had I not seen it dematerialize, or been taken into the cabinet by the form and found the entranced medium there; but I have never seen a single instance of transfiguration, unless the double of the medium be considered as such. The fact that Mrs. Fairchild stands outside, by the cabinet, during the séance, in full view of the audience; that at the Berry Sisters', and at Mrs. Sawyer's, the spirits lead the medium out of the cabinet; that at Mrs. Fay's the forms often take the visitors into the cabinet and show them not only the medium but the materialized control,—are things which the skeptic will find very hard to explain. If they are not evidence of the existence of these phenomena, it is difficult to understand what evidence is.

To a sensitive person, with even a limited experience, the character of a séance is easily determined. There is always in [130] the true materialized forms a decided lack of some of the elements that make up the magnetism of what we call real life; something not easily described, but readily perceived by a person thus constituted. To such a one, neither a confederate nor a personation by the medium can pass undetected.

[131] CHAPTER II.
EXPOSURES OF MEDIUMS.

There have often been sensational reports circulated claiming to be "exposures" of materialization, but when traced to their origin they have generally been found to be unreliable, and never the result of careful study or scientific investigation. The ungentlemanly and in some instances brutal conduct of the parties engaged in the "exposures" has been such as to discredit their statements, and in no case have they produced evidence that would be considered valid in any court.

[132] If it be true that the garments used to clothe the forms are materialized and dematerialized in the cabinet, any sudden disturbance of the magnetic conditions of the circle might arrest the process of dematerialization, leaving the draperies intact. Persons not understanding this would naturally charge fraud upon the medium, on rushing into the cabinet and finding them there. This has led some mediums to submit to a thorough examination of their clothes before entering the cabinet, going so far, at times, as to allow themselves to be dressed entirely in dark clothing, without a particle of white upon them, and giving every opportunity to prove that there were no concealed draperies in the room. These arrangements, while taking up valuable time that otherwise would have been devoted to the séance, have never interfered with the manifestations.

[133] The most serious and perhaps the most generally believed charges made against these séances is that confederates are used to personate the forms. Passing by the many knotty questions which cannot possibly be explained on the theory of confederates, and considering it in a business point of view, there are difficulties connected with such an arrangement that might in the end prove disastrous.

A employs B to personate, at one dollar a séance. B finds that A is making money, and, being rascally enough to engage in such work, would have no scruples in demanding, under threats of exposure, the lion's share of the proceeds.

A is completely in his power, and has no alternative but to submit. This, and the outside pressure which would be likely to be brought to bear upon B to make public the fraud, would render it almost [134] impossible to carry on the deception for any great length of time.

Again, there are often from fifty to sixty distinct individual forms appearing at each séance, requiring as many confederates to represent them. As the circle is rarely composed of more than twenty-five persons, would it pay to keep so many actors for so small an audience? If people who listen to these accusations would reflect for a moment, they would see that the theory of confederates is not a very plausible one, and it might do much toward relieving mediums from the unjust suspicions to which, through lack of understanding on the part of the public, they are more or less obliged to submit.

All honest mediums will cheerfully do all they can to satisfy the public that there is no deception, and that the cabinet and its surroundings are such as to [135] preclude the possibility of confederates. Any other arrangements are unnecessary, and, to say the least, suspicious. These things are new and strange to most people, and they very naturally expect strong evidence; and they are right, provided their desire is expressed in a kindly and gentlemanly manner.

Any one at all familiar with these séances cannot help seeing that there are some mediums and their controls who are largely responsible for the feeling of distrust more or less manifested toward the subject. When the question of a confederate is fairly settled (and no one can be certain of his position until it is done), and two forms appear at the same time; or when you can be taken into the cabinet by a form, and shown the entranced medium, it is self-evident that one of them is a materialized form, and not a personation by the medium. It needs no [136] argument to settle this, no matter how much it may conflict with pre-conceived notions.

I have quoted from Chief Justice Jacolliot's work on Occult Science in India, to prove that there is no connection between these manifestations and what is called sleight-of-hand.

There is, however, a more important fact conveyed in his statements, corroborated by other writers upon this subject, showing the perfect fairness with which these mediums, or Fakirs, submit to tests, courting the most thorough and exhaustive investigation, even trusting themselves, while in a trance, without any protection, to the honor and good faith of those around them, repeating at request the experiments, again and again, to satisfy that there is no deception about them.

This is strangely in contrast with our mediums, who as a rule shrink from anything [137] of the kind, and are disposed to regard any request of that nature as a direct imputation upon their honesty.

If materialization means anything besides dollars and cents—if it has a mission to perform—it is to enlighten and educate the people upon one of the most important subjects that has ever engrossed the mind.

The lack of openness and confidence on the part of many of the mediums, or their managers, creates a feeling of distrust which sometimes finds an expression in rudeness on the part of skeptics, and leads those who are confident of the genuineness of a part of the séance to be impressed with the idea that there are things connected with it that are dishonest.

There is no difficulty in tracing the source of this feeling. Everywhere like begets like, and as long as this state of [138] feeling exists there will be a lack of harmony in the circle, with more or less disturbance.

It may be that these things are inseparable from the newness of the manifestations among us, and will disappear when mediums are more freely developed in our homes, and the séances assume less of a commercial character.

While no apology should be made for fraud in these séances, we have no right to make charges that cannot be sustained. Every medium is bound, in justice to the audience, to see that the cabinet and its surroundings are so arranged that the appearance of fraud is, as far as possible, avoided.

Lack of experience, want of perception, or ignorance of a subject, gives no authority to assume that it is a fraud. The eagerness with which the press circulates reports of imposture finds its excuse, [139] not in a manly defence of the truth, but in a morbid disposition to cater to the whims and caprices of the public. Those who accept such statements without investigation may possibly become victims of a worse delusion than that which they fancy they are condemning in others—a delusion born of ignorance and self-conceit.

[140] CHAPTER III.
PUBLIC SÉANCES.

No comparison can justly be made between different mediums. All are excellent in their way. The preference that is given to one over others is mainly due to personal feeling, to likes and dislikes, which must always find an expression among individuals of different tastes.

In some séances the strength of the manifestations is largely exhausted in the production of forms. In others, the social and affectionate element predominates. Where there are from fifty to sixty materialized forms appearing at a sitting, it is hardly to be expected that much time can [141] be given to the interchange of thought or the expression of feeling. Such séances are, as a rule, mere touch-and-go occasions.

The strength of the circle is often exhausted in combating the ignorance and prejudice of the audience, and the higher and more delicate phase of materialization is lost sight of.

Many condemn public séances on account of the mixed audience and the conflicting elements that surround the medium. These things are, at present, a necessity, being the only means of educating the masses.

The time has not yet come when, through a more general acceptance of the truth of materialization, it can be transferred to the domestic circle, where it properly belongs, and where its best results will be obtained. Not until the flush of excitement necessarily arising from the [142] strangeness of the phenomena has subsided, and the investigator has settled in his mind the facts of materialization, is he capable of forming an intelligent opinion on the subject.

Thousands of persons, through their experience, have reached that point. Whether they advance beyond this will depend upon the character of the séance, the strength of the manifestations, and the purely affectional bearing toward these beings.

Séances should be classified: the first, for primary education, for facts and evidence to convince skeptics; the second, for the more advanced investigator. Into this latter class no skeptic should be admitted. Such an arrangement could not interfere with the patronage of mediums, but on the contrary would enhance it, for there comes a period in the progress of the investigator when, finding that he [143] cannot advance, he will retreat or seek some other field for investigation. The public séance, as now constituted, must, from the nature of its surroundings, remain more or less stationary.

There are séances that are pitched on so low a key that when the investigator passes from a state of doubt into a full knowledge of the truth of materialization, he will instinctively leave them for a more genial atmosphere; for it is in vain to expect that coarse, mercenary, untruthful mediums can avoid impressing more or less of their natures upon the spirits who come through their organisms, or that mainly spirits like themselves will be attracted to them. The more intelligent investigators are beginning to realize this, and those mediums who have lost the sense of their high calling, and degraded the séance to a mere show, will, under the inevitable law of progress, find themselves [144] supplanted by a better element. Mediums are being developed everywhere, and in the near future there will be no lack of noble men and women who will gladly come to the front with their divine gifts.

If we accept the idea that passing to the other life does not essentially change the character of the man, that his peculiarities remain the same, we can account for many things in the séance-room that appear to be simply acting,—performances which have no other object than to attract the audience, to show what power the spirits can acquire under conditions which seem impossible to us.

Considering the state of feeling with which many persons enter the séance-room, it is not singular that they are sometimes treated to what seems to be deception. The spirits, perceiving the condition of the minds around them, act very much as they would if they were [145] still on this side of life. Thoughts are things, which appear to them very much as solid substances do to us. If, instead of attempting to remove them, they can accomplish their object by going round them, they feel themselves justified in doing so. They act very much, at times, as children would under similar circumstances; and, until they obtain complete control over the form that encases them, they cannot express themselves with much force. They are as children learning to walk, to think, and talk through a medium that is new to them.

A simple, childlike bearing, blended with the warmest affection, is the only element that enables them to progress and meet us upon the highest plane of thought.

[146] CHAPTER IV.
THE ATTITUDE OF SCIENTISTS.

The world is indebted to scientists for their clear arrangement of and deductions from what others have discovered; for, as a rule, they are not inventive. Hasty in condemning everything new, their timidity and lack of generous bearing toward what seems to conflict with their materialistic theories are conspicuous.

Nothing can be more unscientific than the attitude of most of them toward this subject. Obliged in the past to antagonize the despotism of the old Theology, they have themselves become despotic. [147] Condemning dogmatism, they assume a dogmatic bearing toward everything that does not square with their pre-conceived notions. Walking with faces toward the ground, they refuse to look up, or admit the existence of anything beyond matter; denying the possibility of spirit, and claiming that the earth contains within itself the "promise and potency" of everything that is or has been.

Against this sweeping claim may be opposed the fact that, in the light of a purely scientific analysis, the earth gives no promise of the living beings that cover its surface; that it creates nothing, furnishes nothing except the environments or clothing of the beings that for the time find their abiding-place here.

When scientists are confronted with materialization, they deny it without investigation, or refuse to examine it unless they can dictate their own conditions, and [148] yet no class of men understand better than they do the necessity of adhering closely to the laws governing any operation in nature, if it is to be fairly studied. The course that has been and is now being pursued by the two scientific bodies supposed to be investigating this subject must necessarily lead to failure. Individual members may be more or less impressed with the reality of the phenomena, but no report worthy of the subject will ever be made by either society. The ridiculous farce enacted by the French Academy of Science in their report on Mesmerism, will probably be repeated here.

It has been charged upon me that I am not a scientist, and that my methods are not scientific,—all of which, if their implied definition of science is correct, I admit. I have had the fairness, notwithstanding my skepticism, to lay aside my [149] prejudices and study this subject purely in relation to itself, and not in connection with pre-conceived ideas. The facts which I have presented have been attested by competent witnesses; and until scientists have made themselves familiar with them, their allegations amount to nothing. The course which I have pursued in studying this subject is far more sensible and scientific than a denial without investigation.

The editor of one of the ablest scientific journals has well said, "Science having no methods by which it can experimentally determine that man has a spiritual nature distinct from the material, it follows that it must be incompetent to throw light upon the nature of that which is unrecognized or unknown."

The testimony of scientists in such matters cannot be considered of any more value than that of any other careful investigator; and if we take into consideration [150] their materialistic views, it is dealing liberally with them to concede that much.

Science accepts the theory of molecules and atoms, and declares matter to be indestructible. These little molecules set in motion produce the phenomena of life. When they get tired and refuse to climb one above another, like acrobats in a circus, then there is death. It is all very simple, and any one can understand it,—a little alkali thrown into some acid,—a rapid effervescence,—the atoms are disturbed and seek to hurriedly arrange themselves into a different position,—they have performed the fantastical dance of life, and all is over!

Upon this theory scientists have endeavored to account for the creation of everything. If they have found anything else they have not declared it. The trinity of Molecules, Atoms, and Motion is the keystone of the whole structure [151] which for centuries they have been trying to build up.

As science takes nothing for granted, it would be interesting to learn when and where they found these little atoms, which no microscope, however powerful, has ever revealed. Before scientists insist upon the denial of the existence of that spiritual force which organizes and individualizes all forms of life, it might be as well for them to settle the question, What is matter?

I do not assert positively that these beings are spirits; for it may be said, in a scientific point of view, I have no right to do so; but I do assert that the facts warrant beyond a question the conclusion that they do not belong to what we call the earth-side of life,—that they are not automatons, lay figures, or effigies, but are living, breathing, intelligent beings, with thoughts, feelings, and passions [152] strictly human; that they come out of invisible space, and depart in the same way. In the language of Professor Crookes, "Nothing is more certain than the reality of these facts. I do not say that they are possible, but I say that they *are*."

[153] CHAPTER V.
PUBLIC OPINION.

When Mesmer appeared in Paris, exhibiting his claims to Magnetism, he was ridiculed, and treated as a humbug. The French Academy of Science, after due consideration, pronounced Mesmerism a fraud. This was the more remarkable from the fact that many of the experiments in Mesmerism are so simple that a child can demonstrate them to the entire satisfaction of an unprejudiced person. Many years afterward, in 1831, the French Academy of Medicine, through a report of its Committee, reversed this decision.

[154] So far as we know, these are the only efforts that have been made, until within a few years, by any scientific association, to investigate this class of phenomena. Both in Europe and this country it has been treated with contempt, and for more than a hundred years condemned by pseudo-Science as nothing more than a hallucination produced by a diseased condition of body or mind.

I was present at the Massachusetts Hospital, many years ago, when the elder Warren, knife in hand, made mock passes over his patient, ridiculing to his students the idea that any one could be entranced or rendered insensible to pain by what was called Mesmerism; and yet the existence of the Mesmeric force or fluid is one of the most remarkable discoveries ever made. It has been known for thousands of years, by the Hindoo philosophers, as "the pure Agassa Fluid" [155] that penetrates and permeates all objects, whether animate or inanimate. It controls the social relations; is the secret of that influence which one person exerts over another; and is the connecting link between the seen and the unseen worlds, enabling spirits, whether in or out of the flesh, to produce all the phenomena known as "spirit-manifestations."

If we except the writings of Deleuze, Townshend, Gregory, Dr. Elliotson, and a few lesser lights, Mesmerism has been kept before the public mainly by a class of itinerant lecturers who, despairing of a more considerate hearing, have, in order to retain their hold on their audience, degraded it to a mere burlesque.

The history of Mesmerism forms no exception to all discoveries that have marked the progress of man from a state of barbarism to the present time. The old stubble chokes and prevents the new [156] crop of grain, unless it has been turned under. The acceptance of anything with which we are not familiar depends more upon the mental condition produced by pre-conceived ideas than upon any evidence necessary to sustain it. The progress of public opinion is like the march of a great army; it camps at night upon ground occupied by its videttes in the morning. When Spiritualism began to attract attention, the opponents of Mesmerism, not understanding its true character, abandoned their hostility to it, and accepted it as an explanation of the new phenomena. Mind-reading, Telepathy, everything possible, was brought forward to explain away this supposed evidence of another life. And, in a somewhat different form, the same thing is taking place in regard to Materialization.

If we eliminate from it the idea of spirits, and attribute to man alone this [157] wonderful power, we disarm scientific as well as sectarian opposition, and the possibilities of man, the influence of mind over matter, become a legitimate subject for study. But no matter how exhaustive your investigations of Materialization may have been, the moment you suggest that spirits may have something to do with it, it becomes unscientific, and, in the judgment of certain persons who have assumed the right to control public opinion, you are instantly transformed from an honest student into a "crank"!

In view of the obstacles that Conservatism is always throwing in the way of Progress, one may be pardoned for a certain kind of admiration for cranks. They have, at least, the courage of their convictions, and in this respect, if for nothing more, may become popular, for the crowd always throw up their hats, [158] whether right or wrong, to the plucky man.

Is courage, then, so rare a thing that we are forced to applaud it even in the bulldog?

Public opinion is the despotism of a republic. It is astonishing what cowards it makes of decent men; the fear of being laughed at is the terror of society; the assertion of manhood, the expression of an honest opinion, the love of truth,—everything goes down before it.

My ministerial neighbor throws theological brickbats at me because I choose to study a subject which he has not the courage to face, and which, if not a reality, he lied about in his last funeral sermon, when he told the mourners that their "dear friend is not dead, but still living and hovering around them."

Shall we allow these attacks, and not [159] remind him that, if he knows anything, he must know that the Christian religion is an outgrowth of paganism; that there is not a cardinal point in his theology that is not as old as the Hindoo Pagodas; that the idea of another life, imperfectly outlined in the Bible, was taken from a religion founded upon occult manifestations; that He whom he calls Lord and Master not only taught healing by laying on of hands, but exemplified Materialization in the transfiguration on the Mount, and in his bodily appearance to his disciples, after his death, in a room with closed doors?

At every séance there are more or less clandestine visitors, who shrink from letting their best friends know anything about it. At one, I met an old acquaintance, who was surprised to find me there, and begged me not to give him away. He had obtained a seat under an assumed [160] name, partially as a test, he said, but mainly on account of his position in society; he did not care to be known to visit such places. In the course of the séance, a beautiful female form came briskly out into the middle of the room, and, stretching her arms toward him, said, "Father!" As he did not respond, the controlling spirit, calling him by name, said, "that lady is for you!" He stepped forward, and, to his astonishment, found that it was his daughter. He said afterward that the recognition was perfect. This was his first séance, and, unless Materialization becomes popular, it may be his last. That he told his wife about it there seems to be no doubt, as she has been a frequent visitor ever since. I fancy him in his dressing-gown and slippers, reclining in his armchair, smoking his cigarette, anxiously awaiting her return, that she may relate to him the [161] touching manifestations of affection she has received.

Traces of these phenomena have always, in one form or another, been present in the world. In India, for thousands of years, they have furnished the foundation of a religious belief, which, like all other religions, has been perverted and used as a means to blind and control the common people.

The danger of its being accepted as authority through a blind reverence for what is supposed to be supernatural, instead of affectionate and intelligent companionship, is sufficient reason why its true import should be thoroughly understood. Whether it be a power in man, the laws of which are unknown, or a direct emanation from another life, it requires the most serious consideration. Shall it receive the attention it deserves, or shall we turn our backs on it, till, like a [162] rising tide, it overwhelms us with a flood of ignorance and superstition? It will not do to ignore it; already its influence is sweeping far and wide.

Scientists may sit supinely on the summit of their intellectual conceit, insisting that it "will not be much of a shower;" still it swells and rolls on, sapping and undermining the whole system of social and religious thought. Sects and creeds crumble in its pathway. All hopes of a scientific evidence of a life after death are centred in these manifestations.

The issue is a plain one; there can be no middle ground. Either Spiritualism or Materialism triumphs. Deal with it as you may; if it is from the other side of life, it cannot be overthrown. In some form or other it must be met.

Shall we not, in the interest of humanity and of what purports to be an important truth, lay aside our pre-conceived [163] notions and prejudices, and treat this subject as we would any of the common things of life, earnestly endeavoring to get at its true meaning?

Millions of honest people have witnessed these things in their own homes, by their own firesides. Against what they have seen and know there is no argument.

Time will show whether the public have sufficiently advanced to grapple healthily with Materialization and its spiritual surroundings.

[164] CHAPTER VI.

CONCLUSION.

It has been heretofore stated that everything known as Spiritualism is due to pure Magnetism.

Magnetism may be classed under three heads: Terrestrial, Aerial, and Ethereal or Spiritual Magnetism. These are only different modes or grades of expression of the same thing; and may be compared, in their order, to earth, air and ether;—heat, force, and light;—or root, stock, and flower in plants.

Ethereal Magnetism is the medium of thought, as is clearly proved by what is sometimes called telepathy, or mind-reading, and by well attested facts of communication [165] between persons widely separated. It is also known to Mesmerizers that, when they have established magnetic relations between themselves and their subjects, they can often control them without reference to distance.

Outside of the domain of this subtle fluid, there can be no connection between the seen and the unseen worlds, or between any of the individual forms of life. More attenuated than Electricity, it holds the same relation to life that Terrestrial Magnetism holds to the grosser particles of matter. It enables what we call intellectual force to command and control all forms.

Through it, Thought, which is the Principle of everything, builds and unbuilds; clothing itself in material garments, and filling the earth with countless millions of individual beings, made visible to our outward senses.

[166] The process by which this is accomplished is the same, whether done instantaneously or extending through a series of years. Materialization, then, is only the manifestation of a law everywhere acknowledged, with this difference: the external forms, under a superior force and intelligence, are more quickly wrought.

It is the question of time, more than anything else, that challenges our skepticism. That which we call progress, or evolution, is only so many steps by which mind exerts itself, with increasing force, over matter. We are in the habit of regarding matter as a solid substance; whereas, in its primitive state, it is invisible. It is only by different combinations, in its aerial form, that it becomes solid. In a fluidic state, it probably pervades all space. In this condition, spirits, it would seem, have power to condense it and shape it at pleasure.

[167] Existing as individual beings, complete in their organization, many of them are able, under certain conditions, to draw from their surroundings sufficient matter to clothe themselves in garments, for the time being, as substantial as any forms in life.

I have witnessed the processes of materialization and of dematerialization in the middle of the room, several feet from the cabinet,—have taken hold of the hands of these beings, and gone down with them to the floor, until the last things that disappeared were the hands that were in mine.

I have been taken into the cabinet by one of these forms, and, with my left arm around the form (to all appearance as solid as my own), have put my right hand on the entranced medium, and while in this position have seen a white, luminous cloud rise slowly from the side of the [168] medium until it reached the height of nearly six feet. I could have passed my hand through it without resistance. In a few seconds it condensed into a human form that cordially greeted and shook hands with me, having a hand as substantial as my own. It was the form of "Auntie," the control, who greeted me with "How do you do? What do you think of this?" At the same time, there were many hands patting me on the head and shoulders.

All this occurred in a cabinet where a confederate was impossible. Was I deceived,—laboring under a state of hallucination? Not if I now have or ever had any knowledge of myself.

I have studied these things as quietly as I would have studied a statue or a picture; have not been satisfied with witnessing them once, but have had them repeated many times, that I might feel certain that I had given them a thorough investigation. [169] If I have been mistaken, those who come after me will have small chance of better success. I have stated some things positively, because I know that they are true, and can be scientifically demonstrated.

We may discover and accept the conditions that best enable these beings to reach and communicate with us, thereby extending our knowledge and our association with them, but neither our observation nor what they may tell us will enable us to comprehend what our experience has not fitted us to understand.

At best we have only established our pickets on the other side of the river. The problem of life still remains unsolved.

The erroneous ideas so generally entertained regarding beings of another life render it important that we should fully understand that no one, whether on this or the other side of life, can set aside the laws necessary to our individual growth.

[170] The assimilation of thought; the gestation of ideas, the mental digestion which is analogous to the process of physical growth, must ever remain the source of a healthy development. To abandon this to the dictation of authority, whether real or supposed, or to accept anything in violation of these laws, only leads to disorder and mental dyspepsia.

What we most desire does not always come; but in its place, often, something unexpected and surprising. The power which operates suffers no dictation or control; and, like the reflection of an object in water, the phenomena become distorted the moment the magnetic currents are disturbed.

Forced, by the accumulation of facts that cannot be set aside, to acknowledge the existence of these beings, they are, nevertheless, shrouded in mystery. That they are from the other life is more than [171] probable; no other theory will, in the long run, be found tenable. Whether they are our departed friends and relatives must be determined by the exercise of those faculties which enable us to settle the relations of objects in this life. While they exhibit no feelings of selfishness or jealousy in their associations with us, the same cannot always be said of "the control." For some reason which we do not understand, but which may be a necessity, the controlling spirit of the séance exercises a more or less <u>despotic</u> power over the manifestations; sometimes denying the privilege of manifestation, and forcing back spirits who have been accustomed to appear at other séances. In other words, there seems to be a good deal of human nature in their make-up, and the likes and dislikes of the medium or manager, are often shared by "the control."

[172] While the theory is correct that the medium is nothing but the instrument through which the spirits are evoked, there can be no question that his or her mental and moral atmosphere affects the quality of the manifestations.

Your personal relations with the medium are known to the controlling spirit, and if the medium is prejudiced against you, you are, in most cases, debarred from any satisfactory results. On the other hand, your relations to these beings are known to "the control," but not necessarily to the medium,—never unless the controlling spirit thinks best to communicate them.

What you learn of the character of these beings depends upon your personality,—the magnetic <u>atmosphere</u> that surrounds you. Many of them, if they are able to penetrate your atmosphere, are so exhausted by the effort that they [173] cannot talk much with you; while others, overcoming all obstacles, are able to throw themselves around you with all the abandon of childhood, talking freely, and often so fast that it requires the closest attention to follow them. In such cases, however strong the resemblance may be to the medium in the outward form, the mental characteristics are as different as it is possible to be between any two individuals.

I have refrained from saying much about the quality of these manifestations. It is a matter upon which there must always be a wide difference of opinion. Every one will find *himself* more or less reflected in them. It is the inevitable law of association. "You are a cheat and a scoundrel!" said an enraged man to my friend. "I know it," was the prompt reply; "it is the rascality and cussedness in you that have called it out. [174] I never was conscious of it until I met you."

No selfishness, deceit, or diplomacy avails with these beings; what you truly think and feel, your moral atmosphere, makes or mars your relations with them. Until you can learn to meet them in perfect confidence, you can know nothing of the beauty which emanates from them.

Materialization is denounced by the learned and the ignorant, and in both cases the denial springs from the same cause. It is a fair illustration of high life with the bottom turned up; both classes meet on the same plane. It is also bitterly condemned by a class of Spiritualists whose brains are saturated with trance and inspirational communications. In their conceit, the little they know is the whole world to them.

As a rule, all nations and tribes hold in some form or another to a belief in the [175] continued existence of man after death. However desirable such a belief may be, it is generally admitted that it rests entirely on faith, there being no substantial evidence by which it can be scientifically demonstrated. In both the Old and New Testaments are records of occult manifestations similar to what has been related here, but the materialistic tendency of science has long since caused them to be regarded as Oriental fictions.

In the materializing séance come, for the time being, living, breathing, intelligent, human forms, that are not confederates or personations by the medium. If not beings from another life, what are they? The probability, or even possibility, they offer of scientific evidence of the existence of man after death, commends them to the serious consideration of every intelligent person.

It is not a difficult task, nor one requiring [176] a great amount of labor, to determine that these forms are distinct embodiments. To settle this is, however, only the A B C of the matter. To learn what these beings are, and their relations to us, requires the most patient investigation and the most delicate and far-reaching exercise of the mind. Facts, in themselves, unless they suggest something higher, are of little consequence. They derive their importance solely from their connection with some general law around which they are grouped.

While I have stated positively that at Mrs. Fay's no confederates are used, and that the forms that have come to me are not personations by the medium, yet, in the *legal* definition of the word, I do not *know* who or what they are. I have my convictions, based upon what is satisfactory evidence to me. I do not ask any one to accept my theories, but upon what [177] have been stated as facts there need be no controversy, since any one who will give the matter the same attention can verify all that has been said.

To deny the facts without an investigation, on the ground that they are impossible, can have no weight, for it has been truly said by Arago that "outside the domain of pure mathematics, the word impossible has no meaning."

I have imperfectly related only a few of the many hundred strange things that have come under my observation, selecting them at random without any special regard to order. The same may be said of the thoughts expressed; their value, if they have any, will be found in the closeness with which I have pursued the investigation. My experience has extended over more than a hundred séances, and to have given them in detail would have exceeded my time.

[178] These things are open to any who will approach them honestly. Let us hope that some fair-minded specialist, whose brain is not lumbered with the debris of old ideas, will yet be able to lift the veil that surrounds them.

I feel confident that I have exhausted almost every conceivable test necessary to establish the reality of these wonderful apparitions. Some of these tests, in the light of a more extended experience, now seem very absurd. Ridiculous as they must have appeared to these beings, they were never vexed, nor showed any impatience with my ignorant and unreasonable demands, but either met them squarely or playfully turned them aside. My investigations have been confined mostly to Mrs. Fay's séances, for the simple reason that here the cabinet and surroundings were known to me to be above suspicion, and from the beginning greater facilities [179] for study were granted me than elsewhere. Such is the skeptical nature of my mind that if I had been obliged to conform to the rôle of an ordinary visitor, I should, in all probability, have never been fully convinced of the truth of materialization.

In dealing with a subject so new to the mass of people, it is hardly to be expected that it will be accepted on the testimony of any one. Facts, however clearly stated, will have but little weight with those who have had no practical experience. Fortunately, the rapid increase in the number of mediums, both public and private, is bringing these things within the reach of every one.

If what I have stated be true,—if the experience of others shall prove that I have not been deceived,—then the whole system of ethics must undergo a complete revolution. Man will no longer be regarded [180] as an animal, confined to earth, but a direct emanation from a superior intelligence, holding in his nature a dual existence, connecting him at one and the same time with both the seen and unseen worlds.

There is no estimating the influence which a realization of these things, rightly understood, would have upon the moral and social condition of society. What has been held in the past as a vague and uncertain belief, would be supplanted by knowledge; and the skeptical tendency of modern thought would be checked by a fuller sense of the inspirational and spiritual nature of man.

The dread of death, throwing a gloom over the domestic circle, would glide away as the darkness of night disappears before the coming morn. The parting of friends and relatives would find its compensation in renewed companionship and [181] the perfect consciousness that there is no real separation.

For the fullness and tenderness with which these beings have overwhelmed me with demonstrations of regard, promptly responding to every reasonable request, I am under the deepest obligations. As I go back in my mind over the various séances which it has been my privilege to enjoy, I linger fondly over the stately form and affectionate bearing of what claimed to be my wife; the rich girlish nature of Bertha, with her marvellous beauty of expression; and the tender pleadings of one who must be nameless here, begging that I would bring those she loved nearer to her.

All along the pathway of my investigations glow a thousand things never to be forgotten. Who shall say the gates are not ajar, and that our loved but not lost ones are not passing to and fro?

[182] Poor in spirit and weak in affection must they be who can meet these beings as I have met them, and not feel that there comes, from the association with them, a richer and fuller life.

Transcriber's Note:

Punctuation has been standardised. Changes to the original have been made as follows:

Contents
Personification by the Medium of Materialized Forms *changed to*
Personification by the Medium, or Materialized Forms

and

Séance at the Berry Sisters in Boston *changed to*
Séance at the Berry Sisters' in Boston

Page 98
With outstreched arms they beckoned me *changed to*
With outstretched arms they beckoned me

Page 136
may conflict with preconceived *changed to*
may conflict with pre-conceived

Page 170
ever remain the source of a a healthy *changed to*
ever remain the source of a healthy

Page 171
exercises a more or less depotic power *changed to*
exercises a more or less despotic power

Page 171
the magnetic atmostphere that surrounds *changed to*
the magnetic atmosphere that surrounds